WEB DESIGN BASICS

Todd Stubbs
Brigham Young University
Karl Barksdale
Technology Consultant, Provo, Utah

THOMSON
COURSE TECHNOLOGY™

Australia • Canada • Mexico • Singapore • Spain • United Kingdom • United States

THOMSON
COURSE TECHNOLOGY ™

Web Design BASICS
by Todd Stubbs and Karl Barksdale

Sr. Vice President:
Chris Elkhill

Managing Editor:
Chris Katsaropoulos

Sr. Product Manager:
Dave Lafferty

Development Editor:
Rose Marie Kuebbing,
Custom Editorial Productions

Production Editor:
Anne Chimenti,
Custom Editorial Productions

Marketing Manager:
Kim Ryttel

Associate Product Manager:
Jodi Dreissig

Print Buyer:
Denise Sandler

Production:
Patty Stephan

Design:
Abby Scholz

Compositor:
GEX Publishing Services

Printer:
Banta

Disclaimer
Course Technology reserves the right to revise this publication and make changes from time to time in its content without notice.

ISBN 0-619-05964-8

Get Back to the Basics...
With these *exciting new products*

Our exciting new series of short, programming and application suite books will provide everything needed to learn this software. Other books include:

NEW! Internet BASICS by Barksdale, Rutter, & Teeter
35+ hours of instruction for beginning through intermediate features

0-619-05905-2	Textbook, Soft Spiral Bound Cover
0-619-05906-0	Instructor Resource Kit
0-619-05907-9	Review Pack (Data CD)

NEW! Microsoft OfficeXP BASICS by Morrison
35+ hours of instruction for beginning through intermediate features

0-619-05908-7	Textbook, Hard Spiral Bound Cover
0-619-05906-0	Instructor Resource Kit
0-619-05909-5	Activities Workbook
0-619-0507-9	Review Pack (Data CD)

NEW! Microsoft Office 2001 Macintosh BASICS by Melton & Walls
35+ hours of instruction for beginning through intermediate features

0-619-05912-5	Textbook, Hard Spiral Bound Cover
0-619-05914-1	Instructor Resource Kit
0-619-05913-3	Workbook
0-619-05915-X	Review Pack (Data CD)

Microsoft Works 2000 BASICS by Pasewark & Pasewark
35+ hours of instruction for beginning through intermediate features

0-538-72340-8	Text, Hard Spiral Bound Cover
0-538-72411-0	Text, Perfect Bound, packaged with Data CD-ROM
0-538-72342-4	Activities Workbook
0-538-72341-6	Electronic Instructor's Manual Package
0-538-72343-2	Testing CD Package

NEW! Web Design BASICS by Barksdale & Stubbs
35+ hours of instruction for beginning through intermediate features

0-619-05964-8	Text, Soft Spiral Bound Cover
0-619-05966-4	Electronic Instructor's Manual Package
0-619-05977-X	Review Pack (Data CD)

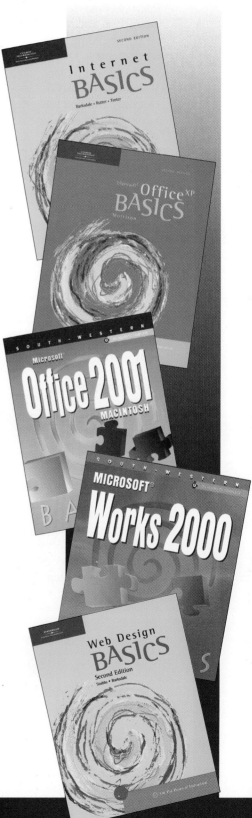

How to Use This Book

What makes a good text about the Internet? Sound instruction and hands-on skill-building and reinforcement. That is what you will find in *Web Design BASICS*. Not only will you find a colorful and inviting layout, but also many features to enhance learning.

Objectives— Objectives are listed at the beginning of each lesson, along with a suggested time for completion of the lesson. This allows you to look ahead to what you will be learning and to pace your work.

Step-by-Step Exercises—Preceded by a short topic discussion, these exercises are the "hands-on practice" part of the lesson. Simply follow the steps, either using a data file or creating a file from scratch. Each lesson is a series of these step-by-step exercises.

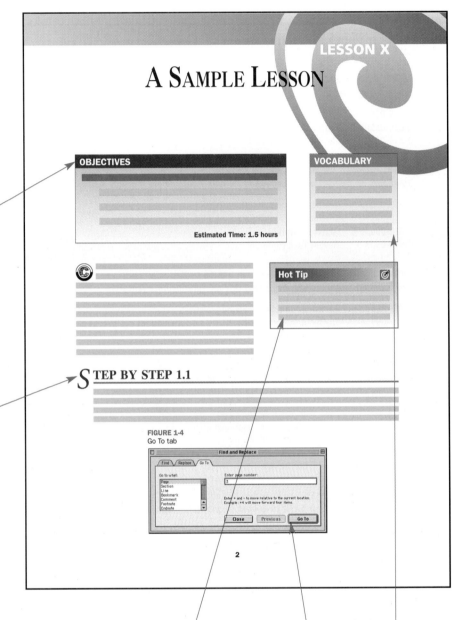

A SAMPLE LESSON

LESSON X

OBJECTIVES

Estimated Time: 1.5 hours

VOCABULARY

Hot Tip

STEP BY STEP 1.1

FIGURE 1-4
Go To tab

2

Marginal Boxes— These boxes provide additional information about the topic of the lesson.

Vocabulary— Terms identified in boldface/italic throughout the lesson and summarized at the end.

Enhanced Screen Shots—Screen shots now come to life on each page with color and depth.

How to Use This Book

Summary—At the end of each lesson, you will find a summary to prepare you to complete the end-of-lesson activities.

Vocabulary Review—Review vocabulary terms presented in the lesson.

Review Questions—Review material at the end of each lesson and each unit enables you to prepare for assessment of the content presented.

Lesson Projects—End-of-lesson hands-on application of what has been learned in the lesson allows you to actually apply the techniques covered.

Critical Thinking Activities—Each lesson gives you an opportunity to apply creative analysis and use the Help system to solve problems.

Lesson **X**   Unit Sample   Intro Excel   **3**

SUMMARY

VOCABULARY*Review*

REVIEW*Questions*

PROJECTS

CRITICAL*Thinking*

SCANS

INTERNET*Milestone*

SCANS—(Secretary's Commission on Achieving Necessary Skills)—The U.S. Department of Labor has identified the school-to-careers competencies.

Special Feature Boxes—These boxes provide interesting additional information about the Internet.

PREFACE

The magic of the World Wide Web has caught the imagination of millions of people. What is this magic? How do *you* make this kind of magic?

For some, the magic is having the equivalent of the huge library at their fingertips. For others, it's the ability to control the computer's screen in a world where the screen often controls them. For most people, it's that they don't have to be a professional magazine publisher, newspaper reporter, graphic artist, or celebrity to get their Web page seen. In fact, unlike other media, you don't have to be a "somebody" at all. Anyone can create a Web page!

Design Makes the Difference

That certainly is not to say that everyone can do it well. There's a difference between knowing the technical elements of HTML and creating attractive and functional Web pages. How do people do it well? What's their secret?

Well, it so happens that it's not a secret, and it's not magic. It's design.

Design is that part of the production of a Web site (or an automobile, or a book, or a work of art, or any creative endeavor) that occurs primarily in the mind of the creator before any part of the physical creation has begun. It is the precursor to all great creative activity.

A natural inclination for someone creating a new Web site or page is to open an HTML editor and begin inserting tags. Although you certainly will want to know something about HTML before you attempt to develop a complex Web site, making it magic is a function of how much effort you put into planning before the HTML coding starts—in the design.

Creating a Design Document

To guide your work, this thought process we call design must be recorded somewhere. This recorded thinking is collectively called a *design document*. The design document is important if you are creating a Web page all by yourself to help you stay on track. But if you are working with others, a design document is vital to communicate your creative thinking to them.

That is what this book is about—how you can do the design work necessary to create beautiful, purposeful Web sites.

Organization and Features of the Text

Web Design BASICS has been written so that your Web design skills can be cultivated and enriched. The Step-by-Step sections are fully illustrated and easy to follow, allowing you to master the basics of an exciting Web design career.

The text is divided into nine interactive hands-on lessons:

Lesson 1—What is the World Wide Web? introduces the design medium called the World Wide Web; its structure, organization, and the tools used to explore it.

Lesson 2—Building a Web Site teaches you the importance of planning, constructing, and testing a Web site.

Lesson 3—Information Design discusses the principals of audience, message, and purpose prior to developing a design document that will organize your Web design work as you proceed.

Lesson 4—Interaction Design asks you to determine how Web site visitors will navigate your site and how they will interact with the information you post online.

Lesson 5— Presentation Design helps you plan the visual aspects of your Web pages, starting with thumbnail sketches and proceeding to themes for your Web site; applying the principles of unity, balance, and proportion.

Lesson 6—Preparing your Text asks you to define your audience, your message, and the purpose of your written text prior to developing the written messages of your Web site.

Lesson 7—The Whys and Wherefores of Web Graphics asks you to examine how graphics are used as interface elements, becoming part of a Web site's message and enhancing a Web site's theme.

Lesson 8—Beginning HTML Help teaches the fundamentals of HTML, applying document formatting, and text style tags.

Lesson 9—From Beginning to End (and More...) reviews the previous eight lessons and asks you to apply your Web design skills.

Web Design BASICS steps through the basics of Web creation and design. Each lesson includes the following:

■ Lesson objectives to specify learning goals.

■ Estimated time of completion.

■ Vocabulary to introduce new terms used in the lesson.

■ Step-by-Step exercises that teach the basics you need to know.

■ Screen illustrations that provide visual reinforcement of what you're learning.

■ Marginal boxes with Hot Tips, Did You Know?, Notes, Computer Concepts, Net Funs, and other features related to the lesson topics. Extra Challenge marginal boxes challenge you to think a little more about the topic being discussed.

■ Special features such as Internet Milestone, Communication Skills, and Programming Skills provide additional information about designing for the Internet.

The end-of-lesson exercises focus on the reinforcement of the skills you have learned in the lesson and provide a comprehensive review of ways you can apply your skills. The end-of-lesson features include the following:

■ Lesson summary.

■ Vocabulary review of new terms presented in the lesson.

■ Review questions and projects to assess your comprehension of what you have studied.

- Teamwork and Web projects for applying the concepts learned in the lesson.

- Critical Thinking activities that require you to analyze and express your own ideas on a variety of HTML challenges and that meet the SCANS requirements.

The unit review is designed to evaluate your overall comprehension of the lessons. The unit review includes the following:

- Review questions.

- Special SCANS projects to help you master the skills you have learned.

- Critical Thinking activities that will help you apply the skills you have learned in the unit to more complicated situations.

A glossary is provided in Appendix B of the text to provide you with definitions for those tricky HTML tags and terms we all need to learn. Additionally, a glossary is provided at the end of the text of all the vocabulary terms used throughout the book. An index is provided to enable you to more quickly locate specific information.

Software

- Internet Explorer or Netscape Navigator to view Web pages.

- Windows Notepad or Macintosh SimpleText to create HTML documents.

Each of these tools currently comes installed on nearly all standard computers. You may substitute Notepad or SimpleText with a word processor capable of saving text files as .htm or .html documents.

Instructor Resource Kit CD-ROM

The *Instructor Resource Kit* CD-ROM contains a wealth of instructional support that will help an instructor teach *Web Design BASICS*. Read and access the *Instructor Resource Kit* with Internet Explorer, just as if you were surfing live on the Internet. Simply open the begin_webdesign_teacher.htm file using your browser and click your way through the various sections of the *Instructor Resource Kit*.

These files may be copied from the CD directly to a hard drive on a computer or to a network drive. The resources are also available online at *www.Course.com*.

A separate Student Guide can also be accessed online or from the CD. Open the student folder and access the student simulation files by choosing begin_webdesign_student.htm using your browser.

SCANS

The Secretary's Commission on Achieving Necessary Skills (SCANS) from the U.S. Department of Labor was asked to examine the demands of the workplace and whether new learners are capable of meeting those demands. Specifically, the Commission was directed to advise the Secretary on the level of skills required to enter employment.

SCANS workplace competencies and foundation skills have been integrated into *Web Design BASICS*. The workplace competencies are identified as 1) ability to use resources, 2) interpersonal skills, 3) ability to work with information, 4) understanding of systems, and 5) knowledge and understanding of technology. The foundation skills are identified as 1) basic communication skills, 2) thinking skills, and 3) personal qualities.

Projects and Activities in which learners must use a number of these SCANS competencies and foundation skills are marked in the text with the SCANS icon.

TABLE OF CONTENTS

UNIT 1 UNDERSTANDING WEB SITE DESIGN AND DEVELOPMENT

UNIT 2 PLANNING YOUR WEB SITE

UNIT 3 PRODUCING YOUR WEB SITE

UNDERSTANDING WEB SITE DESIGN AND DEVELOPMENT

Unit 1

Lesson 1   2.0 hrs.
What is the World Wide Web?

Lesson 2   3.5 hrs.
Building a Web Site

Estimated Time for Unit: 5.5 hours

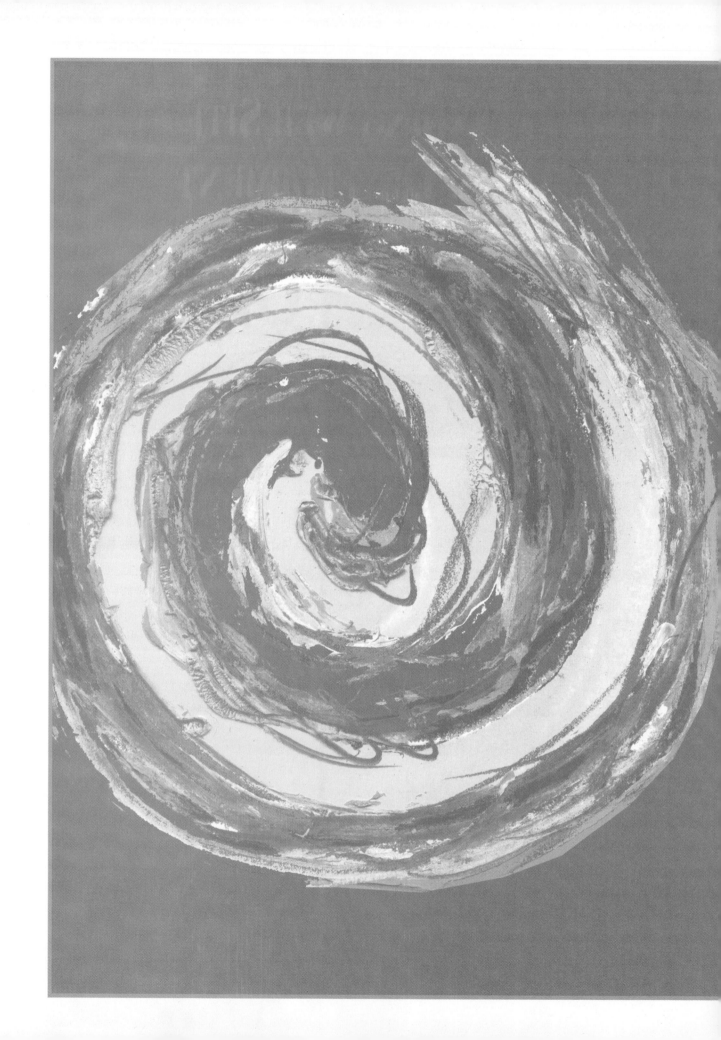

WHAT *IS* THE WORLD WIDE WEB?

How Does the Web Work?

Understanding the World Wide Web

European scientists created the **World Wide Web** (usually just called "the Web") in the late 1980s to share research papers. In four or five years the Web became a new form of mass communications and a powerful way to communicate—much like television and magazines. Using the Web, ordinary people can access millions of pages of information, shop in thousands of online stores, and even share personal hobbies and interests with the rest of the world. In fact, the Web is like a mix between TV and magazines: It is mostly text and pictures like a magazine, but you view it on a screen like television.

One reason the Web is so popular and has grown so quickly is the fact that it is easy to create the files that become a **Web site**. These files are known as **Web pages**; anyone with access to a text editor (like NotePad or SimpleText), a word processor (like Microsoft Word or Corel WordPerfect), or an HTML editor (like MacroMedia DreamWeaver) can create Web pages.

Web pages can be used to sell things, give news, explain ideas, and share opinions. One reason the Web is so popular is because *anybody* with access to the Internet can look at those Web sites—no matter where they are. Through the Internet and the Web, people in virtually every corner of world can share something about themselves or their interests.

When learning to design a Web site it is helpful to compare it to an automobile manufacturer making a new kind of car. The manufacturer doesn't simply start drilling, cutting, and shaping pieces of metal, welding and bolting them together, painting them, and putting tires under them. Building a car requires careful design. Thousands of parts need to be assembled in a particular way. The designers usually start out working on paper (see Figure 1-1). Then they build small models followed by life-sized models made out of clay. Next they build working prototypes of plastic and steel, and finally they make real cars. Design starts on paper (or on a computer) because it is very easy to change things while they are on a sheet of paper or in a computer file. Designers can make lots of changes without much difficulty or cost. By the time a car's design has evolved to a life-sized model, making changes becomes very expensive. Designing a Web site follows many of these same steps. These are the topics of this text.

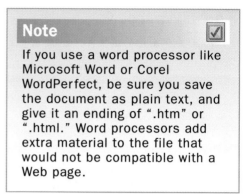

Note ☑

If you use a word processor like Microsoft Word or Corel WordPerfect, be sure you save the document as plain text, and give it an ending of ".htm" or ".html." Word processors add extra material to the file that would not be compatible with a Web page.

FIGURE 1-1
A design and the real thing

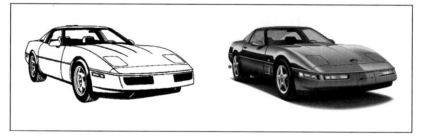

Continuing with the analogy of designing a car, you probably ought know something about driving and roads. Good Web design requires that you know something about the Internet to understand what will work and what won't. For that same reason, you will need to learn a little about how the Web works.

Internet Milestone

THE FIRST HYPERTEXT MACHINE

When was the first hypertext machine thought of? Would you believe 1945? Vannevar Bush conceived of a device, called "Memex," which used photographic technology to link related materials together in what today we call *hypertext*. Though it was never built, the device is the great-grandmother of the Internet, which is based on hypertext. The word *hypertext* was not thought of until much later—by Ted Nelson in the 1960s.

How Does the Web Work?

The Web is part of the *Internet*, a global computer communications network. You may have heard the Internet referred to as an "information superhighway." A highway system starts with a neighborhood street that is probably relatively small, but then connects with larger and faster streets until it comes to a freeway or highway. Businesses are often found next to larger streets so they can serve larger numbers of people; houses are often by smaller streets—just large enough for you and your neighbors.

In a city, the streets connect all the buildings; in a network, wires and other types of connections connect all the computers. The Internet starts with a small, simple network—often a Local Area Network (LAN)—like a neighborhood. Computers in a network use the network's connections like streets to send messages and information to each other and to share services such as printing. As shown in Figure 1-2, these small networks are interconnected into a larger network, a "network of networks." Interconnect all of the networks in the world and you have the Internet (it is like an international highway system).

FIGURE 1-2
A network of networks

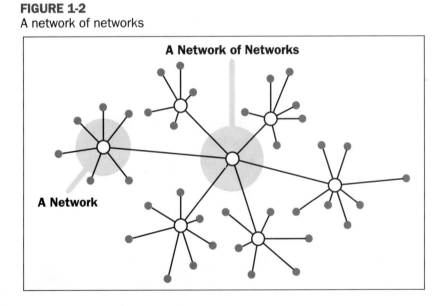

When connected to the Internet, all you have to do is key in the Web address (called a *URL*, which stands for Uniform Resource Locator) and your *Web browser* (the program you use to access the Web) contacts the computer where that page is stored (the *Web server*). The server receives your message and sends the page by breaking the information up into little bundles called *packets,* each of which has *your* computer's address on them. These packets "wander" the Internet, looking for your computer. If a packet gets lost, your browser will tell the server to send it again. Finally, as all the packets begin to reach your browser, it assembles them into a Web page and displays the page to you. The parts of a network and paths to the Internet are shown in Figure 1-3.

FIGURE 1-3
The parts of a network

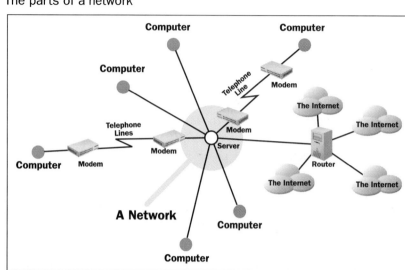

STEP-BY-STEP 1.1

1. Get together in a small group of about four or five classmates. This group represents a LAN. On one side of a small piece of paper (about 1/4 of a sheet is fine) write a short note to someone else in the group.

2. When everyone in your group is done writing his or her notes, tear the notes up into four or five smaller pieces. Don't make the pieces so small they cannot be written on. (These torn-up papers represent Internet packets.)

3. On the back of each torn-up piece of paper, write the name of the person for whom the note is intended. (The name represents the URL.) Also, write two numbers: one signifies what number piece it is, and the other number tells how many total pieces there are (for example, "Packet 3 of 7"). Place all the pieces in a box, hat, or other container with the pieces from everyone in your group.

4. Pass the hat from person to person. Everyone will draw out a "packet" from the hat. If it has your name on it, you can keep it and use it to begin to assemble your note. If not, put it back and pass the hat to the next person.

5. Continue passing the hat around until all "packets" have been delivered and thus all notes assembled.

6. Keep the papers for the next activity.

As you may have guessed, Internet packets don't really wander aimlessly. Other network computers help send the packets on to their destinations and help locate other routes when one becomes broken or clogged with traffic. These computers are called *routers*. A router is a computer that tells packets which way to go—like a traffic cop. If one path breaks down, the routers help the packets find another way to reach your computer.

> **Internet**
>
> Current links to most Web sites presented in this book can be found on the Web Page Design home page at *webdesign.swep.com.* Remember that a Web address can change at any time. An address given in this book as an example may no longer be valid. If that happens, access this book's home page, or do a search for a similar site.

STEP-BY-STEP 1.2

1. Gather together all of the slips of paper again. Mix up the slips for the entire class.

2. Identify four or five people in the class to act as routers. Their job will be to pass the packets in the right direction—to the right LAN or group. For example, if they receive a packet with Paulo's name on it, they need to pass the packet in the direction of Paulo's LAN group.

3. The teacher will place some of the packets on each desk. Pass the slips as before, but when one reaches a router, have that person route the paper in the correct direction.

4. Keep passing until everyone has received all of his or her packets and can assemble their messages once again.

Your Connection to the Web—The Browser

Your connection to the Web comes from a type of software called a Web browser that interprets and displays the Web pages to you—in other words, it puts the packets together. In this section you will learn about how a browser works.

Net Concept

Because of differences in the way browsers work, some designers may actually create two or more separate versions of every page. The pages include programming that enables them to tell what kind of browser is requesting the page, and then send the appropriate version. Often, a text-only version is one of those options because it is viewable on any browser.

Extra Challenge

Imagine how slow the Internet would be without routers! What would happen if you tried Step-by-Step 1.2 with the entire school without routers? How long would it take for every person to receive his or her packets? How much do routers improve that situation? How might you modify Step-by-Step 1.2 for a whole school to finish it quickly? What could you do to play the game for a stadium full of students? Can you see the kinds of problems that crop up when millions of people are using the Internet?

Internet Milestone

WHY DOES THE INTERNET WORK THAT WAY?

The scientists who invented the Internet made it so that the self-addressed packets can find their way to your computer even if one or more of the "highways" is broken down. Why? This protocol was invented for the military during the Cold War when the United States and Western Europe were concerned that the Soviet Union might start a nuclear war. The scientists wanted to make sure that messages got through even if there was a nuclear attack and parts of the network became inoperable. That's one of the reasons the Internet is so flexible.

A Web browser is the software that you use to retrieve and view Web pages. A dictionary definition of browsing is "glancing through a book or the books of a library for casual reading." Browser is a good name for this kind of software because it allows you to follow *hyperlinks* to see new documents. (Hyperlinks are places in a Web page's text or pictures you click on to automatically jump to another page on the Web.) Most other forms of computer access to information require you to either search for information or look it up in an index. On the Web, you can do those things too—using a *search engine* to search for Web pages that have things you're looking for, or using a **Web index** to look up information by category. These are not, however, the main way you use a browser.

In a browser, hyperlinks to other Web pages are typically noted by being underlined and differently colored, or set apart in some other way, so you can see them clearly (see Figure 1-4). When your mouse pointer passes over these hyperlinks, it turns into a hand to let you know that you can click on them and move to another page.

> **Note**
>
> The instructions and illustrations in this text use Microsoft Internet Explorer. They can, however, be easily adapted for use with Netscape Navigator, Netscape Communicator, or any other browser because browsers all have basically the same elements. Open your browser by double-clicking on its icon (Macintosh or Windows) or by selecting it from the Applications or Internet categories under the Start menu button (Windows).

FIGURE 1-4
A hyperlink

If you decide to go back to the page you just came from, click the Back button (located in the upper-left corner of the browser window on most browsers, as in Figure 1-5), and your computer will jump back (by following the hyperlink). In fact, if you have followed several hyperlinks, you can jump back through them all. Eventually, when you get back to where you started, the Back button will be shaded gray to indicate that you can't click it any more.

FIGURE 1-5
The Back button

In the following Step-by-Steps, you will get to know the parts of your Web browser (and what they do), and you will learn to use a search engine and a Web index.

STEP-BY-STEP 1.3

1. Open your Web browser.

2. See how many of the main elements of the browser you can identify, using the following list. If you need help, refer to Figure 1-6, in which many important parts of Microsoft Internet Explorer (Macintosh version) are clearly labeled.

   ■ The browser's content area
   ■ The address box
   ■ The various navigation buttons
   ■ The status bar
   ■ The animated status icon
   ■ A text-based hyperlink

FIGURE 1-6
Microsoft's Internet Explorer

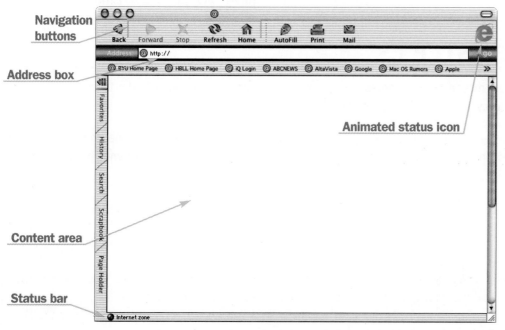

3. In the address box, key the following URL: **www.geocities.com**. Then press **Enter**.

4. Take some time to explore how each of the browser parts work. Leave your browser open for the next Step-by-Step.

Now that you've learned a little about how your browser works, let's try searching the Web for information. To do this we'll go to a true search engine.

S TEP-BY-STEP 1.4

1. Click your mouse in the address box.

2. Delete the current contents and key the following URL: **www.altavista.com**. Then press **Enter**.

3. The AltaVista home page appears with a blank box near the top. This is where you key in what you're looking for. To the side of this blank box is a button that says Search.

4. In the blank box type the words **web page design** and then click the **Search** button.

5. A list of pages that match your search criteria appears. Several of these might be useful to you in this course. Explore them if you like—you can click on the hyperlinks right from the search results page and go to the new pages and then use the Back button to return to the search results page. Leave your browser open for the next Step-by-Step.

AltaVista and other search engines automatically gather information about pages on the Web and maintain records of millions of Web pages. When you use one of these search engines it compares its records to the words you entered. If any of the Web sites match the words you keyed, it puts them in a list for you.

Now let's look at a Web index. One of the most popular Web indexes is Yahoo!

S TEP-BY-STEP 1.5

1. Click your mouse in the address box. Delete its current contents and key the following address or URL: **www.yahoo.com**. Then press **Enter**.

2. You will see a page similar to that shown in Figure 1-7. You can search this one, too, but we're not going to. Instead, click on the link titled **WWW** under the "Computers & Internet" category (in the main section of the window).

STEP-BY-STEP 1.5 Continued

FIGURE 1-7
The Yahoo! Web page

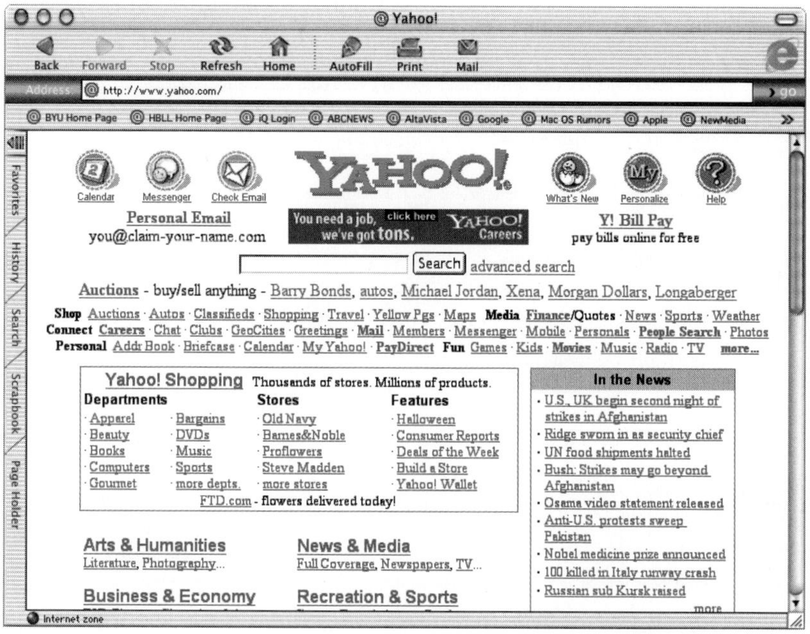

3. Look at the various categories and find one that seems likely to contain information on designing a Web page. Possible category names are: Beginner's Guides, or Page Creation. Browse through some of these categories (by following the hyperlinks and using the Back key to return to the main Category page) to find and review information that may be useful in this course. Leave your browser open for the next Step-by-Step.

Unlike AltaVista, Yahoo! lets Web page owners like you list their Web sites—kind of like the yellow pages of the phone book. When you list a Web site, you tell Yahoo! what categories to put it in. That is why we call it an index rather than a search engine. You can find information by browsing through the topics and subtopics.

An overwhelming majority of Web users use either Netscape Navigator or Microsoft Internet Explorer as their browsers, but there are, in fact, many, many Web browsers. Many of these browsers work very differently, so a Web page that looks great in one browser might look bad in another. Figure 1-7 shows you what the Yahoo! home page looks like when viewed with Microsoft

Internet Explorer (which can display images). In contrast, Figure 1-8 shows you what the same Web page looks like when viewed with the Charlotte Web browser (which displays only text).

FIGURE 1-8
The Yahoo! Web page viewed with the Charlotte Web browser

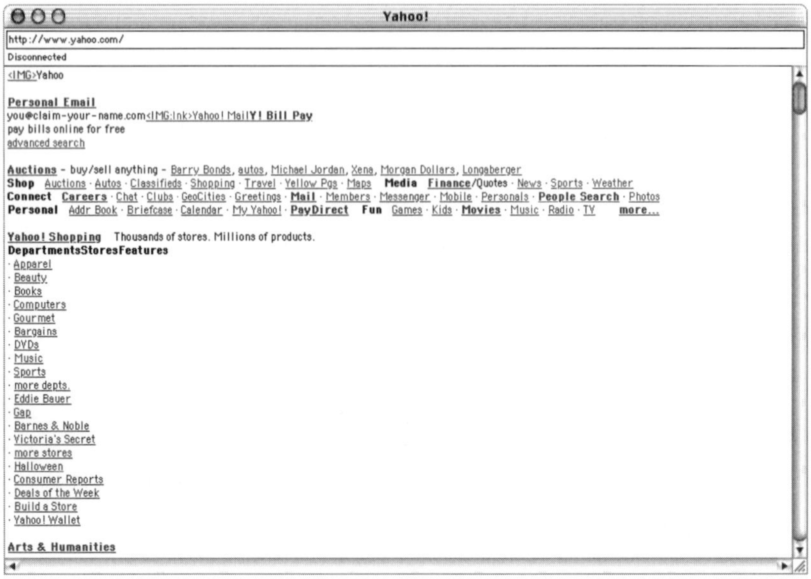

Obviously this is an extreme example of the difference between browsers. Internet Explorer is a graphical browser that is able to display pictures as well as words. Charlotte is a text browser that can only display words. Fortunately, over 95 percent of the people who surf the Web use Internet Explorer or Netscape Navigator, both of which are graphical browsers. In fact, both Internet Explorer and Navigator have a *GUI* (graphical user interface, pronounced "gooey"). GUIs display pictures and allow the use of other multimedia (such as audio and video). They also let you navigate by using your mouse to click on pictures or highlighted words.

Extra Challenge

Which do you think is a better way to look for particular information on Web pages—a search engine or an index? Might you use one for one purpose and one for another? What purposes are best served by search engines and indexes?

Internet Milestone

MOSAIC AND NETSCAPE

The world's first graphical Web browser was called Mosaic. Students and professors at the University of Illinois, Urbana-Champaign, developed it in 1993 for the National Center for Supercomputing Applications (NCSA). Mosaic took the Internet by storm. Within a few months of its release, over 2 million people were using it, and Web traffic had increased by over 300,000 percent!

One of the students who helped develop Mosaic, Marc Andreessen, left the university in 1994 to start a new company called Mosaic Communications. When the people at NCSA complained that they owned the name Mosaic, Andreessen changed the name of the company to Netscape.

As you design your pages, it is good to remember that not everyone accesses the Web through a graphical browser. In fact some Web surfers—such as visually impaired surfers who use text-based browsers with text-to-speech software to "read" the Web pages—will not be able to see any of the pictures on your Web pages.

How Fast Is the Web?

Because computing happens at the speed of electricity, it usually doesn't take long for the Internet packets to find their way to the user's computer. This process is called *downloading*—the process of transferring files from a server to a computer. However, if there is a lot of traffic on the Internet or if your connection to the Internet is slow, you may have to wait while all the packets reach your computer.

The time it takes for someone to download a page over the Web is a function of five factors:

■ The size of the Web page (including the text, all graphics, and so on).

■ The speed of the user's Internet connection.

■ The number of other messages competing for use of the Internet (called Internet traffic).

■ The speed of the Web server's connection.

■ The speed of the Web server.

Typically, the user's Internet connection is the slowest of these, so the faster the user's Internet connection, the faster the Web pages will load. The bad news is that most home users access the Web through a *modem*, which greatly limits download speed. (A modem lets computers use plain old telephone lines to communicate.)

In contrast, if the members of your intended audience are at a large company, a university, or some public schools, they may have a more direct connection to the Internet, which is much faster. In our street analogy, it's as if they have an office right off the highway. Most telephone and cable companies now offer faster services to the Web, such as digital connection lines (DSL) and cable modems. Obviously, the faster the user's connection, the faster he or she will be able to download your page.

STEP-BY-STEP 1.6

1. Key **www.course.com** in the address box of your browser. Once the Course Technology Web site has opened, use the Search box to perform a search using the title of this book or its ISBN number. Information about this book will appear in the Search Results.

2. Click the title of this book.

3. In the page that appears, click **Download Student Files**, and then click **Web Design Basics** under the Student Online Companion heading.

4. Have a watch or clock with a second hand ready. Click on **Timed Web Page 1**. Start timing as soon as you click and see how long it takes for this page to load. Note the approximate time to load.

5. Press the **Back** button.

6. Again, have a watch or clock with a second hand ready. Click on **Timed Web Page 2**. Start timing as soon as you click and see how long it takes this one to load. Note the approximate time to load.

STEP-BY-STEP 1.6 Continued

7. Calculate the difference between the two times to load the pages.

8. Compare the two pages you loaded or look at Figure 1-9. What is the difference between these pages? How much faster did the first page load? Why?

FIGURE 1-9
The speed comparison Web pages

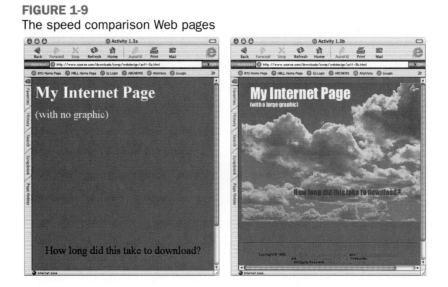
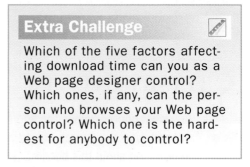

9. Leave your browser open for the next Step-by-Step.

As a Web page designer you cannot control the user's connection. Unless you work for a large company, you usually cannot change the server's speed and you cannot control how much Internet traffic there is. That leaves the size of your page as the only thing you can control to speed up the Web page. The more things you put on your Web page and the larger it is (in bytes), the longer it takes to download—and the longer it takes to download, the smaller your audience will be. Impatient users will simply give up waiting for your page and go off to visit another site.

That means that as a Web designer, you are left with a complicated decision: "Which will increase the num-

ber of my viewers—using this really cool graphic in my site, or doing away with the graphic so the page will download faster?" Often the answer is a compromise between the two: a smaller graphic or a more Web-friendly way to achieve the same "coolness."

Making a Simple Web Page

One of the reasons the Web is so popular is that just about anybody can (and does!) have a Web site. This is because Web sites are relatively easy to create. All you need is a word processor to create your Web pages and someone to serve them. The special codes that make the Web work are called *HTML,* which stands for Hypertext Markup Language.

Some word processors (such as Microsoft Word and WordPerfect) allow you to save documents in HTML format, keeping any formatting you've done to the document. However, for this activity, avoid using those built-in HTML saving options.

STEP-BY-STEP 1.7

1. Open any text editor or word processor. The built-in Windows text processor (NotePad) or word processor (WordPad) or the standard Macintosh text editor (SimpleText) will work well for this exercise.

2. Enter the following text exactly as it appears below. Use the "less than" and "greater than" symbols (usually found at shift-comma and shift-period, respectively) for the angle brackets.

   <HTML>

   <HEAD> </HEAD>

   <BODY>

   Hello,

   my

   name

   is

   [put your name here]

   </BODY>

   </HTML>

3. Save this document as **SimpleWebPage.html** in text-only format and close the text editor or word processor.

4. Open your browser, and use it to view your newly created page. You can open a file by keying the directory location and filename in the address box or by locating it through the File, Open menu commands. When opened, the page you created should look like Figure 1-10.

5. Close your browser.

FIGURE 1-10
Your sample Web page

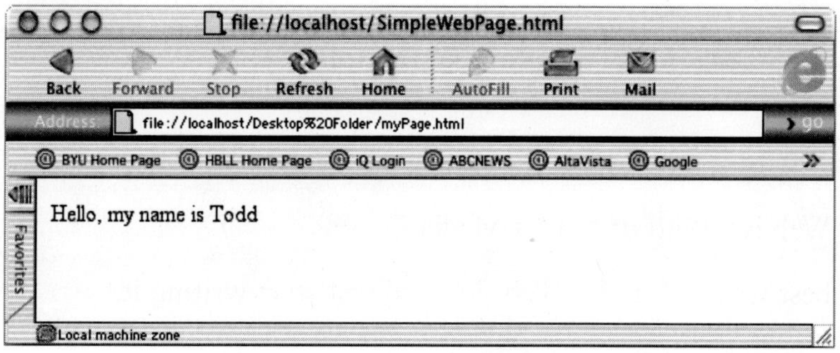

Notice that the file's address in the address box does not start with the usual "http://" but rather starts "file://" or "localhost://" because it is saved on a local disk. Also notice that in spite of the fact that you put every word on a separate line, it all shows up on the same line in the browser.

Though it is a very simple example, all Web pages are fundamentally like this one. They are all made up of text with simple codes inserted that tell the browser how to display the information. The codes in the "angle brackets" (less than and greater than symbols) are called *HTML tags*. HTML is called that because you "mark up" the text with these tags. In Lesson 6 you will learn more about using these tags to create your site.

SUMMARY

In this lesson, you learned:

■ What the World Wide Web is and how it works.

■ To identify the elements of a Web browser and explain how the browser works.

■ To determine how fast a Web page loads.

■ To create a simple Web document.

VOCABULARY *Review*

Define the following terms:

Downloading	Hyperlink or link	Resource Locator)
GUI (graphical user interface)	Internet	Web browser
HTML (Hypertext Markup Language)	Modem	Web index
	Packets	Web pages
HTML tags	Search engine	Web server
HTTP (Hypertext Transfer Protocol)	Routers	Web site
	URL (Uniform or Universal	World Wide Web

REVIEW *Questions*

TRUE/FALSE

Circle T if the statement is true or F if the statement is false.

T   F   1. The Web is a kind of "Mass Media."

T   F   2. The best way to build a Web site is to just start writing it.

T   F   3. The Internet uses the Web to transport information.

T   F   4. A router speeds the movement of packets toward their destination.

T   F   5. All Web browsers can display pictures.

FILL IN THE BLANK

Complete the following sentences by writing the correct word or words in the blanks provided.

1. The acronym "GUI" stands for _____.

2. AltaVista is an example of a Web application that takes text from Web sites so you can search for Web sites, and is called a(n) _____.

3. Yahoo! is an example of a Web application where Web developers list their Web sites so you can look them up, often through a hierarchical list, and is called a(n) _____.

4. Generally, the only thing a Web developer can control that will affect the speed at which his or her Web page opens is the _____ of the Web page and its elements.

5. HTML stands for _____.

WRITTEN QUESTIONS

Write a brief answer to each of the following questions.

1. Why is it important for a Web designer to understand how the Web works?

2. What is the difference between a Web search engine and a Web index?

3. What can you as a Web page author do to make sure that a page loads quickly?

4. When using a word processor to build a Web page, what precautions do you have to take?

PROJECTS

PROJECT 1-1

As a newly hired Web designer for World Wide Widgets, Inc., you have been given the assignment to investigate creating Web pages for the company. The boss, Wendy Widmark, is kind of old-fashioned and is hesitant to move into advertising on the Web. Before she will approve of developing Web pages, she has to understand how the Web works.

Write a memo to Wendy detailing how the Web works and save it as **World Wide Widgets Memo**. Also, create a simple Web page for World Wide Widgets to demonstrate to Wendy how Web pages are built. Save it as **World Wide Widgets Web Page**.

TEAMWORK PROJECT

Form a team of three or four classmates to consider what is required to build Web pages. Start by discussing the following questions:

- Assuming that you could have people from any kind of background or training, what kinds of people would you choose to build a Web site?

- What does the creation of a Web site entail?

With your team, brainstorm all the kinds of skills you can think of that might be needed to build the site. Then have team members select a job title that would be responsible for each skill. Possibilities include an artist, a graphic designer, a computer programmer, a systems analyst, a videographer, a sound engineer, an information designer, or a project coordinator.

Have all members of your group decide which job they would want to perform, and discuss what people in those jobs do and why their contributions to Web page development are important.

CRITICAL *Thinking*

Based on what you know about the Web at this point, write a 100-word essay to address one or more of the following questions.

ACTIVITY 1-1

How important is it for a business to have a Web site?

ACTIVITY 1-2

How important is it for a school to have a Web site?

ACTIVITY 1-3

How important is it for an individual to have a Web site?

BUILDING A WEB SITE

So you want to build a Web site. If you know HTML, you could just start making it, couldn't you? Yes, you could. But it would probably not be a very exciting or easily navigated site. To create a great Web site, the whole process is going to take some work before you ever sit down at the computer. Then, after you've built the site you're going to want to do some things to make sure it's right. Great Web site development happens in three phases: *planning*, *constructing*, and *testing*.

Phase 1: Planning a Web Site

When you adequately plan your Web site you know what your Web site will look like before you start to build it. Planning is like creating a blueprint for a house (see Figure 2-1)—a drawing that tells exactly what the house will look like; where to put the beams, electrical wiring, and plumbing; what kinds of materials to use; and so on. The people who build the house are always looking at the blueprint to figure out how things are supposed to be put together. The blueprint answers most of the questions about building the house. A good Web design is like that.

FIGURE 2-1
Using a blueprint for a house

But where does the blueprint come from? How do you answer all the difficult questions in advance? If you are an architect, you begin by deciding how you want the house to look and why. There are a lot of things to consider when building a house: How many bathrooms do we need? How many bedrooms? How should the house be arranged? (For example, should the kitchen be located right off the living room, or would it be better to have to go through a hall or another room to get to it?) Before the architect ever puts pencil to paper (or nowadays, mouse cursor to screen) a lot of questions need to be asked.

The Blueprint

The approach to building a Web site is very much the same as building a house. You have a lot of questions you need to answer before you will be able to decide what pages to build and how they will be connected together. Once you have the answers to these questions, then "draw your blueprint" in such a way that it answers the questions. In fact, answering all the questions that come up is what makes a good Web design (or blueprint).

Following is a beginning list of some of the questions you might ask yourself before beginning a Web site.

- Who is this Web site's *audience*? Who is it for?

- What is its *message*? What is the Web site about?

- What is its *purpose*? What is it for?

- How will the information in the Web site be organized? (*organization*)

- How will the Web site work? (*interactivity*) How will people get around in it? (*navigation*)

- Will it be easy to use? (*usability*)

- What will it look like? Will its *"look"* complement its message?

The process of asking these questions and writing down detailed answers is called *design*. Design is very often the difference between a good Web site and a mediocre one.

Did you notice that the best way to answer some of the questions might not be with a written answer? For example, the best answer to the question "What will it look like?" may be a sketch. The best answer to the question "How will the information be organized?" may be a diagram and so forth. Each of these forms of communication is called media. Which media or presentation form would best communicate your ideas? Printed words? Pictures? A PowerPoint slide show? A sample Web page? Think about the best way to share your ideas.

STEP-BY-STEP 2.1

1. Using Table 2-1, identify the way each of the questions can best be answered, that is, which media each would be most likely to use. For example, the audience and the purpose might best be defined in words (text), but the look might be best explained in the form of a sketch. Write your answers and be prepared to justify them in a group discussion.

TABLE 2-1
Media for the message?

QUESTION	MEDIA OR THE PRESENTATION FORM THE MESSAGE CAN TAKE
Audience: Who is it for?	
Message: What is it about?	
Purpose: What is it for?	
Organization: How is it put together?	
Navigation: How do you use it?	
Usability: Is it easy to use?	
Look: What does it look like?	

2. Break into teams of three or more.

3. Discuss the forms of media that each team member believes would communicate the required information most effectively.

4. Discuss as a class why you selected the forms you did.

The Breakdown

With the blueprint in hand, you can gather another kind of information. Because the blueprint for a house specifies which materials to use and shows how much of them will be needed, architects can use the blueprint to estimate the total cost of the house. To do this they create a *breakdown*. A breakdown means that you break the project down into small parts and group like things together so you can guess the cost and time for each of them. For example, the breakdown of a house under construction groups all the wood, steel, concrete, and other materials needed and puts them in a table so they can be used to calculate a price. A good builder can look at the breakdown and blueprint and estimate the amount of work to be done and the time it will take to build the house.

An estimate is just an *educated guess*. What is an "educated guess"? Based on the breakdown, it is guessing the money and time needed for each small part, then adding them all together to produce a total estimate. Good estimators usually add a little more, just in case they have misjudged or miscalculated something.

You can do the same thing for a Web site. A good Web design will specify every bit of artwork and programming needed in the Web site. You can guess how much time (and money) each part of the site will take and add them up to estimate the total time you will need to build the site. Why should you worry about time? If you figure out that your cool Web site is going to cost you hundreds of hours of work, you may need to decide if it is really worth it.

In the case of a Web site, time is money. Often no other costs are involved. So, you estimate the time, decide how much each hour is worth, and multiply to obtain your total cost. Table 2-2 is an example of a Web site cost chart that shows the calculations to be performed. Our educated guess is that each Web page will take six hours to build plus an additional three hours to create each picture on each page. The hourly rate used in this example is $17 and we project that we will have 25 hours per week to work on this project.

TABLE 2-2
Calculations for a Web site cost chart

DEFINITION	NUMBER (#) OF WEB PAGES	WEB PAGES DEVELOPMENT HOURS	PICTURE DEVELOPMENT HOURS	TOTAL HOURS
Pages with 0 pix		# pages * 6 hrs=	= 0	Estimated hours=
Pages with 1 pix		# pages * 6 hrs=	# pages * 1 pix * 3=	Estimated hours=
Pages with 2 pix		# pages * 6 hrs=	# pages * 2 pix * 3=	Estimated hours=
Pages with 3 pix		# pages * 6 hrs=	# pages * 3 pix * 3=	Estimated hours=
Pages with 4 pix		# pages * 6 hrs=	# pages * 4 pix * 3=	Estimated hours=
Total Estimated Hours				Total of hours=
Total Weeks to Completion				Hours/25=
Total Cost				# hours * $17=

S TEP-BY-STEP 2.2

1. Imagine the following is true about a proposed Web site. The Web site you are building consists of:
   - 24 Web pages.
   - Some pages have as many as four pictures; some have none.

> **Note** ☑
>
> The word "pix" is short for "pictures."

2. You also know the following to be true:
   - The more pictures, the more time (and money) each page will take to produce.
   - The number of pictures on each Web page is listed in the table below (Table 2-3).
   - The time needed to build and finish each Web page is 5 hours plus another 3.5 hours for each picture.
   - You have 20 hours a week to work on this Web site.
   - You generally charge $15 per hour for this kind of work.

3. Use the Web site cost table (Table 2-3, shown below) to estimate the money and the time required to build this Web site.

> **Did You Know?** 💡
>
> If you are proficient with a spreadsheet program, the best way to calculate this type of information—particularly if you will be doing it often—may be in a spreadsheet application.

TABLE 2-3
Web site cost chart

DEFINITION	NUMBER (#) OF WEB PAGES	WEB PAGES DEVELOPMENT HOURS	PICTURE DEVELOPMENT HOURS	TOTAL HOURS
Pages with 0 pix	7			
Pages with 1 pix	4			
Pages with 2 pix	5			
Pages with 3 pix	6			
Pages with 4 pix	2			
Total Estimated Hours				
Total Weeks to Completion				
Total Cost				

4. You decide that each picture will only take 3 hours instead of 3.5 hours. How does that change the estimate?
   a. Total Estimated Hours =
   b. Total Weeks to Completion =
   c. Total Cost =

STEP-BY-STEP 2.2 Continued

5. Imagine you have some competition for the job. Recalculate the spreadsheet planning to spend only 4.5 hours per page, 3 hours per picture, and at a $14 per hour rate. How would that change the estimate?

   a. Total Estimated Hours =

   b. Total Weeks to Completion =

   c. Total Cost =

6. Imagine that you underestimated the time it would take to develop both pages and pictures. Increase the number of hours spent per page to six and the number of hours spent on each picture to four. At $15 per hour, what would the total cost be?

Phase 2: Constructing a Web Site

Constructing a house requires special skills. You have to know how to select, measure, and cut materials. You have to know how to attach things so they will stay together. You have to know how to use all kinds of tools (see Figure 2-2).

FIGURE 2-2
A house under construction

Constructing a Web site involves the same process. You need to be able to pick materials to use on the Web site. You need to know how to put them together. You need to know how to use tools to create and adapt material for your Web site. You need to know how to put a Web site together so it works.

Houses are made of wood, steel, and concrete, among other things. Web sites are made of text, pictures, and programming. Of course, both houses and Web sites are also made with time and effort.

S TEP-BY-STEP 2.3

1. Select a Web site to look at. Pick a corporate site or a major entertainment site.

2. Estimate the number of pages on the site.

3. Estimate the average number of pictures per page.

4. Use the Web Site Cost Chart from Step-by-Step 2.2 to calculate how much this site would cost to create at $20 per hour.
   a. Total Estimated Hours =
   b. Total Weeks to Completion =
   c. Total Cost =

Putting Things in Order

Another consideration of construction is the order in which things must be done for the building to come together properly. For example, you cannot build the roof until there are walls to put it on. You cannot build the walls until there is a foundation to put them on. You cannot make a foundation until you dig a hole for it, etc. There are more subtle sequences as well. For example, it is always a good idea to have the painters come before the carpet layers. Why? If you do it in this order, the painters can be kind of sloppy and there's no harm done (the spills and overspray will be hidden by the carpet). But if the carpet is already laid, then the painters need to take a lot more care not to get paint on the carpet. This means the painting will take more time and will cost more money.

The same kind of thinking needs to go into the creation of a Web site. Some things are just best done before others.

S TEP-BY-STEP 2.4

1. Revisit and analyze the Web page you examined in Step-by-Step 2.3.

2. Write down all the parts of the Web page on a sheet of lined paper. Leave five or six lines between each of the items on your paper. This list may include such things as text, titles, pictures, buttons, links, and other elements.

3. Consider what kinds of work (activities) would be needed for each of these elements and write them on the lines between each Web page part. For example, text would need to be written, formatted, edited, proofread, and then placed on the Web page.

4. Using the list you created above, write on a slip of paper (or a 3" x 5" card, sticky notes, etc.) each activity or kind of work to be done. As you create these slips, be sure to add to them what object is being worked on. For example, "Edit" may apply to text, programming, or pictures. Make sure you specify which one you are referring to (in other words, "Edit the text").

5. Divide into teams of three or four.

STEP-BY-STEP 2.4 Continued

6. As a group, discuss whether any of the activities need to be performed in a given order. For example, writing text must occur before it is proofread.

7. If they do have a set order, set them vertically in order. If some steps do not need to be performed in any particular order, set them horizontally next to each other, as shown in Figure 2-3.

FIGURE 2-3
Putting steps in order

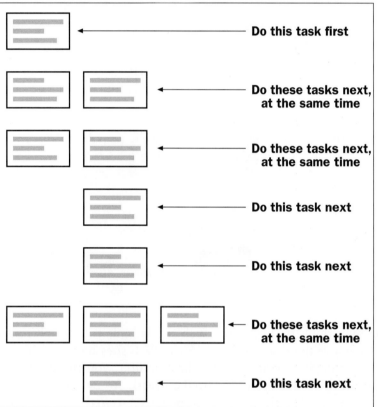

8. Explain to your class why you put tasks in the order you did.

This should give you a pretty good idea of why some things must come before others. Applying the skills you have learned above—breakdown and sequencing of activities—to the creation of your own Web site is an important part of being a good project manager. If you were actually building a Web site, you could now apply what you have learned to begin working on constructing Web pages for your Web site.

Phase 3: Testing a Web Site

Once the house is finished—the doors have all been hung, the toilets and sinks have been installed, it is painted and decorated—it is time to move in, right? Nope. Not quite. Before someone moves into a new house, a person called a building inspector comes and checks out the house and decides whether it is ready to live in (see Figure 2-4). The new owners may also inspect the house to make sure everything has been done the way that they requested.

FIGURE 2-4
Building inspectors for a new house

Likewise, you may think that once the Web site is built you are all finished. Surprise! Not quite. You have one more thing to do: test it. Since Web sites have text in them, you had better check spelling and grammar. If your Web site has pictures, you need to make sure they are the right pictures and that they have been formatted correctly for use on the Web. And the programming that has gone into your Web site needs to be tested to make sure it works like it should. If everything is right, then, and only then, it is ready to be placed on the Web.

Basically, the building inspector checks for two things: whether the house is safe and whether the law (building code) has been followed. A Web site needs three types of testing:

1. **Content testing** (Is everything correct?)

2. **Functional testing** (Does it do what it is supposed to do?)

3. **Usability testing** (Is it easy to use?)

S TEP-BY-STEP 2.5

1. Table 2-4 contains two lists: The list on the left shows the different kinds of testing and the list on the right shows the problems that need to be fixed before the Web site is ready to be released. Draw a line from each of the problems on the right to the category of testing on the left that will find and correct it.

TABLE 2-4
Web site problems and the types of testing that detect them

TESTING CATEGORY	WEB SITE PROBLEM
Content Testing	A misspelled word
	A link does not work
	It is the wrong picture
Functional Testing	It is hard to get to page 3
	A cool "mouse over" does not work
	The site only works with Internet Explorer
Usability Testing	A paragraph is written poorly
	A picture has too high of resolution
	Users cannot tell which things they can click on

2. Discuss your answers as a class.

SUMMARY

In this lesson, you learned:

■ The three phases of Web site production.

■ Two parts of the planning process.

■ What a breakdown is and how it works.

■ Some of the parts of a Web site that need to be constructed.

■ Why some tasks in Web site construction need to happen in a particular order.

■ Three kinds of testing that take place after the Web site is built.

VOCABULARY *Review*

Define the following terms:		
Audience	Interactivity	Organization
Breakdown	Look	Purpose
Content testing	Message	Usability
Educated guess	Navigation	Usability testing
Functional testing		

REVIEW *Questions*

TRUE/FALSE

Circle T if the statement is true or F if the statement is false.

T   F   1. Planning and design are the same thing.

T   F   2. Phase 2, constructing a Web site, requires putting things together.

T   F   3. Use the breakdown to figure out who your audience is.

T   F   4. Phase 3, testing a Web site, is an optional phase—you do not really need it.

T   F   5. Construction requires few, if any, skills.

FILL IN THE BLANK

Complete the following sentences by writing the correct word or words in the blanks provided.

1. Probably the best form of media to describe the organization of a Web site is a(n) _____ .

2. That phase of building a Web site in which you make sure everything on the site is as it should be is called _____ .

3. Probably the best form of media to describe the audience of a Web site is _____ .

4. In _____ testing you make sure all of the parts of the Web site are working correctly.

5. The phase of building a Web site in which you write down all the answers to questions before you actually start to build is called _____ .

6. _____ testing is used to check the spelling, grammar, and accuracy of the material on the Web site.

7. That phase of building a Web site in which you actually collect and assemble all the parts and pieces into the site is called _____ .

8. _____ testing helps you see if the Web site is easy to use.

9. Probably the best form of media to describe the "look" of a Web site is a(n) _____.

10. After you have created a design or blueprint of the Web site, you can do a(n) _____ to see how much time it will take and how much it will cost.

WRITTEN QUESTIONS

Write a brief answer to each of the following questions.

1. What is the value of planning before beginning to construct a Web site?

2. You have heard the common phrase "Time is money." What does that have to do with building a Web site?

3. Why test your Web site?

PROJECTS

PROJECT 2-1

Your Web design company has been asked to design and prepare a bid for a Web site for Theme Parks Unlimited to introduce a new theme park in Texas. From your design phase, you have determined that the site will consist of approximately 100 Web pages with about 5 pictures per page.

Prepare an estimate similar to the one created in this lesson showing approximately how many hours of labor it will take and how much it will cost. Assume each Web page takes 5 hours, each picture takes 3.5 hours, and your rate is $20 per hour. (You can use a spreadsheet program, a table in a word processor, or pencil and paper.)

PROJECT 2-2

Prepare a PowerPoint presentation to help sell your proposal and bid to Theme Parks Unlimited. Imagine that members of your class are Theme Parks Unlimited executives and present your proposal to them.

WEB PROJECT

Congratulations! After reviewing your bid, Theme Parks Unlimited has selected your firm as a finalist to bid on the Web site development job. Your original bid (from Project 2-1) was based on hypothetical numbers. Now you need to do some research to develop a better estimate of the number of pictures on a page and how many pages you can expect in this new Web site.

Look at Web sites for other theme parks. Some suggested sites are:

- www.disneyland.com
- www.disneyworld.com
- www.knottsberryfarm.com
- www.seaworld.com
- www.buschgardens.com
- www.universalstudios.com
- www.sixflags.com

Six Flags originated in Texas; since the theme park for which you are creating a Web site is also located in Texas, you will want to pay particular attention to it. Visit a number of these sites, count the number of pictures on 10 pages, and average them. Then count the total number of pages. (*Note:* Sometimes pictures are broken up to act as buttons or interactive elements. When this is the case, treat them as a single picture for this project.)

Use the information from your review of these Web sites to rework your original estimate to design and build a Web site for Theme Parks Unlimited.

TEAMWORK PROJECT

Discuss with your team which of the three phases of building a Web site is the most important. As a group, prepare an answer to this question to share with the entire class.

CRITICAL*Thinking*

ACTIVITY 2-1

Put yourself in the role of a Web site development company. Consider why it is so important to estimate properly and accurately. What problems might be caused if you underestimated and had to go back to the client to ask for more money? What issues are involved with overestimating?

UNDERSTANDING WEB SITE DESIGN AND DEVELOPMENT

REVIEW *Questions*

TRUE/FALSE

Circle T if the statement is true or F if the statement is false.

T   F   1. A packet is a collection of e-mail messages transmitted over the Web.

T   F   2. A search engine and a Web index are the same thing.

T   F   3. Design is a kind of planning.

T   F   4. A browser is a software program for viewing Web pages.

T   F   5. Downloading is moving data from a server to your computer.

T   F   6. The correct order is design, test, and then build.

T   F   7. A breakdown helps you determine the time and cost of building a Web site.

T   F   8. Testing is essential to assure quality of a finished Web site.

T   F   9. The purpose of the design phase is to construct the Web site.

T   F   10. Navigation refers to how things are put together.

MATCHING

Match the correct term in Column 1 to its description in Column 2.

Column 1	Column 2
___ 1. Usability	A. The network of networks
___ 2. Navigation	B. Transferring files from a server to your computer
___ 3. Audience	C. A user interface that uses graphics
___ 4. Interactivity	D. You click it to see new documents in a browser
___ 5. Breakdown	E. Who the Web site is for
___ 6. Hyperlink	F. A Web page's address
___ 7. Downloading	G. How you compute the cost of building a Web site
___ 8. URL	H. How easy the Web page will be to use
___ 9. GUI	I. The answers to the questions raised by the design
___ 10. Internet	J. How you get around a Web site
	K. How a Web site works; how users work with it

WRITTEN QUESTIONS

Write a brief answer to each of the following questions.

1. What is one thing a designer can do to speed up a Web page?

2. What is a browser, and how do you use one to look at a Web page?

3. What are packets, and how do routers help to move them around?

4. How are HTML tags used to create a Web page?

5. What are some of the questions that are answered in the design/planning phase?

6. What are the pieces in a Web page?

7. What is one kind of testing? What does it test for?

PROJECTS

Use the Web production job described below and the estimation method demonstrated in Lesson 2 to complete the following three projects with estimates and timelines.

- The proposed Web site will have 13 pages. Each page will contain two pictures, except the Welcome page, which will contain one.

- Assume each Web page's programming will take four hours and each picture three hours. Your usual charge for this kind of work is $14 per hour. Round your days to the nearest whole day.

SCANS PROJECT 1-1

In the first estimate and timeline, assume that you will work a standard eight hours per workday. How much will it cost and how many workdays will it take to produce the proposed Web site?

SCANS PROJECT 1-2

In the second estimate, assume that the client considers this a "rush" job, so you are going to put in 12-hour workdays and charge time-and-a-half for any hours over eight. How much more will the second estimate's cost be, and how much faster will you be able to get it done?

SCANS PROJECT 1-3

After hearing your estimates, the client wants to know how much cheaper and faster the estimate and timeline would be if he supplied the pictures ready to insert and just had you do the programming. Calculate an additional estimate and timeline based on a regular eight-hour workday.

CRITICAL *Thinking*

SCANS ACTIVITY 1-1

Five major factors affect the speed of a download. List these five factors in order by how much control the Web designer has (first being the one over which she has the most control and the last being the one over which she has the least control). Explain why you placed each factor in the order you selected.

PLANNING YOUR WEB SITE

Unit 2

Estimated Time for Unit: 8.5 hours

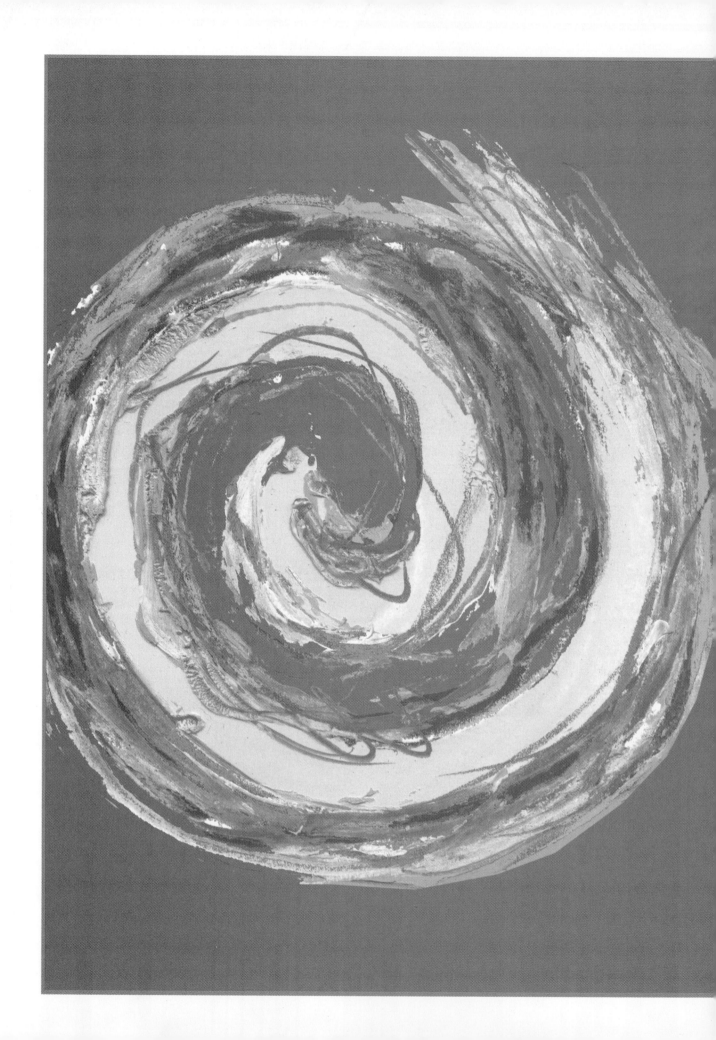

INFORMATION DESIGN

OBJECTIVES

Upon completion of this lesson, you should be able to:

- Identify and document your Web site's message.

- Identify and tailor your information for your Web site's audience.

- Identify and develop your Web site's purpose and scope.

- Structure your Web site's information into a flowchart.

Estimated Time: 3 hours

VOCABULARY

Chunks

Design document

Flowchart

Hierarchical structure

Information design

Linear structure

Mixed structure

Persona

Random access structure

Scope statement

What Is a Design Document?

Great Web sites are not usually built by individuals; they are built by teams with members who have three essential skills:

- Writing
- Computer programming
- Artistic skills

It is nearly impossible to find a single person who can write well, is a great artist, and can program a computer. Instead, companies that make great Web sites will hire several people with different skills and abilities and have them work together as a team to build the Web site.

A *design document* keeps all of these talented people working together effectively. A design document is to a Web site what the blueprint in Lesson 2 is to the building of the house, or what a script is to producing a movie—it guides what happens. A design document outlines the goals of the site and describes or illustrates all its parts. Good design documents contain at least three kinds of information:

- Information design
- Interaction design
- Presentation design

Remember the questions we said you needed answers to in Lesson 2? Well all those questions fall under three types of design.

Information Design

Information design includes these questions:

■ Who is this Web site's audience? Who is it for?

■ What is its message? What is it about?

■ What is its purpose? What is it for?

Interaction Design

Interaction design includes these questions:

■ How will the information be organized?

■ How will the Web site work? What will people do to get around in it?

■ How can I make it easy to use?

Presentation Design

Presentation design includes questions like these:

■ What will it look like?

■ How can I make its look and its message work together?

The first kind of design, information design, often requires a team member who can write well. The second, interaction design, usually needs someone who can program a computer. The third, presentation design, most often needs an artist. Blending writing, programming, and art using information, interaction, and presentation design are the keys to a successful Web site. And, that is exactly the job of the design document.

A design document keeps the writers, programmers, and artists working together well. In this unit we will briefly explore information, interaction, and presentation design. In the process, we will show you how to put them all together into a design document to keep the Web site's development moving forward. In this lesson we will focus on the specifics of information design. Lesson 4 will discuss interaction design. And finally, Lesson 5 will demonstrate how to integrate presentation design into your Web projects.

Information Design

The auditorium is filled with thousands of people, all there to hear you give a speech. Suddenly, you are being introduced! In about three seconds, you will step up to the microphone and begin your speech. Then it hits you: You don't remember what you're there to talk about! You don't remember who these people are, or why they should care what you have to say. Why are you giving this speech anyway?

Sound far-fetched? Sound like a nightmare? Well, it happens every day on the Web. Thousands of people visit Web sites looking for something interesting or important to them. Instead, they find aimless, meaningless, disorganized, and sometimes downright confusing information.

What is wrong with these Web sites?

There might be any number of reasons why a Web site doesn't work. However, it is our experience that the designers of most poor Web sites neglected to answer three important questions before they started to build the site:

■ What is this Web site about? (What is the *message* of this site?)

■ Who is this Web site for? (Who is the *audience* for this site?)

■ What is this Web site for? (What is the *purpose* of this site?)

The answers to these three questions make up the Web site's ***information design*** (see Figure 3-1). An information design helps your Web site avoid mediocrity. When you figure out the answers to these questions, you will want to write them down so you can refer to them later. These written answers are the first part of your design document.

FIGURE 3-1
Information design is made of message, audience, and purpose

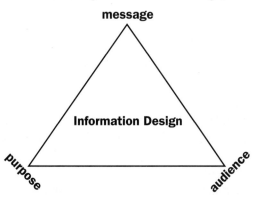

Among these three parts of information design, which one comes first—the audience, the message, or the purpose? Actually, sometimes it is one and sometimes it is another. The following examples will help. They show how other Web site developers faced these three design issues.

■ The purpose of a bookseller's Web site is to make money selling books; therefore, making money (the purpose) is the seller's first thought, followed closely by the books he is selling (the message), and finally the people who buy books (the audience).

■ A student shared her university's sports history (the message) online. Those interested in the site included sports fans and alumni of the university (the audience). The site was used to help promote interest in the university's sports program (the purpose).

■ Another Web site supports the families of people who suffer from cancer. The audience (the families of cancer sufferers) was thought of first, with the purpose in mind (to comfort families) using the message (in-depth information about cancer research).

As you can see, it is very hard to separate these three design questions—they're all connected. If the bookseller's Web site focused so much on making money (its purpose) that it didn't show off the books very well (the message), or didn't show respect for its customers (the audience), it wouldn't sell many books. The bookseller would lose customers, and the Web site's original purpose—to make money—would be ruined. Good design requires you to think carefully about all three questions.

Discovering a Message for Your Web Site

As a Web page designer, your first task is often to figure out what your message is and research it. What? You say you don't know what to create a Web site about? Well, this next activity will help you figure that out. First, you'll brainstorm a list of topics you're interested in, then refine that list to one or two good ideas.

STEP-BY-STEP 3.1

1. Brainstorm with classmates and write down ten topics in which you are interested. These can include hobbies, interests, pets, favorite school subjects, your family, work, or just about anything. If you are developing your site as a partnership or team, develop ten topics with your partner or team.

2. Copy the items in your list in the order in which they most interest you (or your team), with the most interesting topic first. (If you get stuck trying to decide which item should be first, compare them two at a time, putting a mark next to the one that wins each pairing. The one with the most marks is first, the one with the second highest number of marks is second, and so forth.)

3. Look at the first topic in your list and ask yourself, "Can I create a great Web site based on this idea or topic?" If you don't feel you can build a Web site about your first topic, continue down the list until you have at least one topic that can make a great Web site. You should choose something that (1) you either know or are willing to learn about, (2) you are interested in, and (3) is not too narrow and not too broad. If necessary, have your instructor help you decide which topic would be most suitable for a Web site.

4. Your chosen topic or subject will become the message of your Web site. Talk with your instructor or team members about this message. Discuss whether it would be a good topic before you finally decide to develop your Web site around it. Make sure it is a topic you will enjoy spending many hours working on.

5. After you have discussed your message with your instructor, open your word processor and key the heading **Message**. Under this heading, write a description of your message statement beginning with the words **This Web site will** _____. This will be the beginning of your design document.

6. Spend some time (three to ten hours outside of class) researching your message. Take your time and learn as much as you can. Naturally, the Web is one great resource to draw from. You may also want to spend some time in the library or talking to others who know about your subject. Write down what you learn and where you learned it.

STEP-BY-STEP 3.1 Continued

7. After the message statement in your design document write a short reference note for each significant source of information you find so you can locate the information again if you need to. Put these references under the heading **Resource List**. Make a short note about what each reference contains so you can remember it in the future. Figure 3-2 shows a design document that has been started for a university sports history site.

FIGURE 3-2
Start your design document with a message statement and a resource list

8. Save your design document and leave it open for the next Step-by-Step.

Who Is My Web Site's Audience?

After you have decided what your Web page is going to be about and have gathered information about it, you will want to figure out whom you want to have view and read your pages. This is called your *audience*. Your Web pages need to be tailored to meet the needs and wants of your target audience.

Extra Challenge

Some believe that the Web can be used to give any message at all. Can you think of any message that can't be communicated by way of the Web? Can you think of any that shouldn't be communicated through the Web? What is it about these messages that make the Web an inappropriate medium of communication?

An audience is a group of people who have something in common. Whatever it is they have in common should be somehow related to the message of your Web site. Here are some ideas of things that audiences can have in common, just to get you thinking:

- Where they live ("people from Jefferson City, Missouri")
- What they do for a living ("carpenters")
- A hobby they share ("people who build model trains")
- The style of clothes they like ("people who wear purple shirts")
- A kind of music they listen to ("people who listen to jazz")
- A language they speak ("Tagalog-speakers")
- Some kind of food they like ("people who eat sushi")
- A cause that they feel strongly about ("people who believe in gun control")
- Some combination of things ("people from Jefferson City who build model trains")

To identify the audience for your Web site, you must identify what it is that the group has in common with your Web site. For example, it is not enough to say "my Web site's audience consists of people who like fish." That might mean you are creating a site about keeping fish as pets. It might also mean your site is about ways to prepare fish to eat. Or it may even refer to people who like Phish—the rock group. In that case, your audience will include anyone who likes that group's music (or maybe people who *don't* like it). To identify your audience, you must decide what its members have in common AND what makes them unique—what makes them different from other, similar groups.

Another way to see if your audience description is clear enough is to come up with a *persona* that represents your audience. A persona is a description of a person, real or fake, who is a member of the group. To make the persona seem real, fill in lots of details about her and explain how she is a member of the audience. For example, using the sports Web site example, "Susan (not a real person) is an example of a person from our audience. She is an 18-year-old woman who loves sports and is a freshman at University of Northern Utah. She is from a small town near the university and used to watch UNU football and basketball games with her family. She herself plays tennis and hopes to make the UNU tennis team next year. She is a business major and is quite competitive, having taken fifth place in state high school tennis finals last year." Can you see how creating a persona helps make the audience more real and alive?

STEP-BY-STEP 3.2

1. In your design document, describe your audience with a paragraph. This is called an *audience statement*. Be specific enough that your audience will not be confused with any other group. One way to do this is to demonstrate the characteristics the audience shares and what sets it apart from other, similar groups. The statement should be about 35 to 50 words long.

2. Under the heading **Audience**, insert your audience statement between your message statement and your resource list. Your audience statement should state clearly what the audience has in common with your Web site's message. For instance, in Figure 3-3 the audience includes fans of a university sports program.

STEP-BY-STEP 3.2 Continued

3. After the Audience heading, add the heading **Persona** and a paragraph to describe an individual persona for a member of your audience. Give as much relevant detail as will make the persona seem real and complete to you. This paragraph could start with an introductory statement like: "Jeremiah is an example of a person from this audience. He…". Figure 3-3 shows the design document with the audience and persona statements added.

FIGURE 3-3
Insert your audience and persona statements into your design document

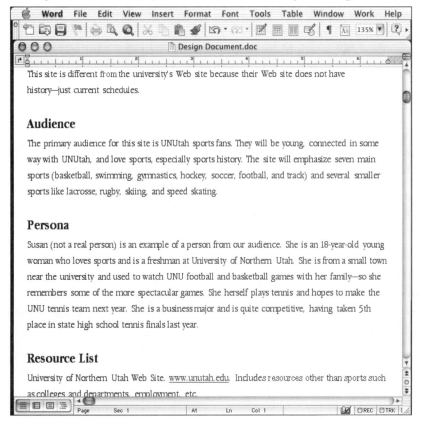

4. To make sure you've been thorough enough, share your audience and persona statements with a partner or classmate, and allow him or her to share his or her statements (if you are working in a team, do this within your team). Discuss whether what you've written could be confused with any other group or audience than the one you've identified.

Questions you and your partner or team may ask each other are:

- Does this audience statement include people who *wouldn't* be interested in this Web site?
- Are there other people who might want to look at this Web site who are *not* included in the audience statement?
- Is the persona a good representative of the audience?

5. Make corrections to your audience and persona statements as needed and resave your design document.

What Is My Web Site's Purpose and Scope?

Purpose

It is essential that you make the purpose of your Web site clear *before* you begin creating it. A "purpose" that is too broad or too narrow can make your site ineffective. You need to be very specific in your definition of purpose.

Let's say you have identified your target audience as people who like to eat sushi—a Japanese-style dish that includes raw fish and vegetables. What might a Web surfer who likes sushi be looking for when he or she comes across your site? Why would he or she be searching the Web for sites about sushi in the first place?

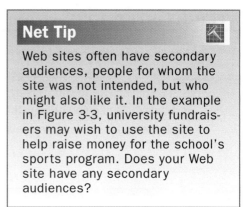

Net Tip

Web sites often have secondary audiences, people for whom the site was not intended, but who might also like it. In the example in Figure 3-3, university fundraisers may wish to use the site to help raise money for the school's sports program. Does your Web site have any secondary audiences?

- Maybe the surfer is hungry and is looking for places that serve sushi in his or her town. In that case, a *directory* of local sushi restaurants would fill the need.

- Perhaps he or she is planning to learn how to prepare sushi and wants to know how it is done. In that case, a *"how to"* Web site, one that teaches the skill of preparing sushi, is the best type of site.

- Maybe he or she just caught a fish and is wondering whether this particular fish can be eaten raw. In that case, an *informational* Web site about the types of fish that can be used for sushi is what is needed.

- It's also possible that you are building a Web site that is all about sushi—that is, it includes all three of these topics and others.

Notice that your Web site's *message* (content) and what you know about its *audience* can help you define your *purpose*. The more you know about what your audience knows and expects, the easier it is to craft a statement of purpose.

One method many professional designers use to understand their purpose is an *audience analysis*. In Step-by-Step 3.3 you will perform an audience analysis to help you make your Web site's purpose clear.

Communication Skills

WHO IS MY AUDIENCE?

Following are some generalized examples of a few Web page audiences:

- People searching for other Web pages and information (examples: search engines like Google and Web indexes like Yahoo!)

- People interested in your company, school, or organization (examples: company Web sites like Apple Computers' home page, school sites like Union High School's home page, or organization sites like the Web site for Future Business Leaders of America).

- People interested in a particular product, topic, or class (examples: software product Web sites like the Microsoft Office home page, a Web site for people who like cats, or a Web site for people taking an algebra class at your high school).

- Your instructor or employer (examples: a Web page you created for a class assignment or a Web report you were assigned to prepare for your company).

- Your friends and family (example: a personal Web page).

- You (example: a "bookmark" page that includes links to your favorite Web pages).
    While the importance of the audience, the message, and the purpose vary from site to site—and they all are interconnected—the audience is, in most cases, the most significant consideration when designing Web pages.

WHAT DO THEY ALREADY KNOW?

If you don't already know what your audience may already know, you will tend to provide too much or too little information. For example, it would be silly for you to create a Web page whose audience includes six-year-olds that contains the following sentence: "A central problem in theoretical discourse is our lack of a common metatheoretical language and framework within which we can categorize and debate diverse positions. (W. R. Shadish. 1998) Most six-year-olds don't know enough to understand that sentence. (Taken out of context as it is, you probably don't either!)

Thinking about what your audience already knows will keep you from making these two common mistakes: talking down to them and talking over their heads. Talking down to your audience means that you're not only telling it things it already knows, you're making its members lose interest in your Web site because they feel like you're showing off. Talking over their heads is like that sentence in the preceding paragraph—they just won't understand it. In either case, they will quickly decide that your Web site probably won't meet their needs.

STEP-BY-STEP 3.3

1. Conduct an audience analysis. If possible, interview members of your intended audience. (If you can't talk to representatives of your audience, you may need to make some educated guesses about it.) You could prepare a form with questions on it (a survey) or you could interview potential members of your audience one-on-one. Ask them what they already know about your topic, and find out what they expect to see in a Web site about your topic. Questions may include:

   - What kind of information would cause you to visit a Web site on this topic?
   - What do you already know about this topic?
   - What do you want or need a Web site on this topic to do or say?
   - How would you like to see the information?
   - What parts of the message are of greatest interest to you?
   - What benefits could come from a Web site on this topic?

2. Review your message and audience statements and include or change anything of importance you learned while talking to them.

3. Write one or more paragraphs (at least 35 words) explaining the primary purpose of your site. Insert this purpose statement under the heading **Purpose** in your design document between your description of the persona and your resource list, as shown in Figure 3-4. Be clear, concise, and direct in your purpose statement.

FIGURE 3-4
Purpose and Audience Background in the design document

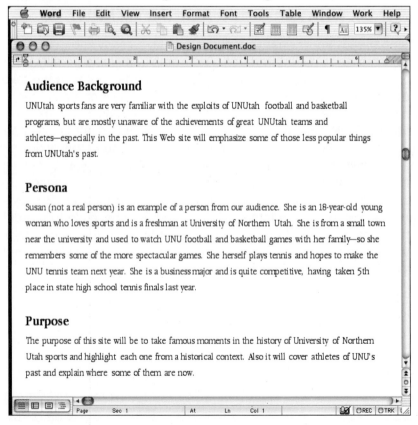

STEP-BY-STEP 3.3 Continued

4. Write one or more paragraphs explaining what your audience already knows. This will be called the audience background statement. Under the heading **Audience Background**, insert this information between your audience statement and your description of the persona, as shown in Figure 3-4. This information will be useful for your Scope statement, which you will do in the next Step-by-Step.

Scope

Once you have a pretty good idea of what your audience already knows, you can begin to talk about what your message will and won't cover—listing what you will and will not talk about on your Web site. This is called a *scope statement*. Without a scope statement, it is easy to get caught up in your subject and write too much! This can make it hard to finish your Web site on schedule. Or, without guidelines, you could write too little. Detailing your scope will keep you focused on the important aspects of your topic.

STEP-BY-STEP 3.4

1. Make two lists in your design document under the heading **Scope** (see Figure 3-5). Insert these lists right after your message statement. List three to five things that your site will present. Then make a list of three to five things that your site won't discuss—things that come under the general topic, but that you don't intend to cover. Use these two lists to help focus your later work and its limits.

FIGURE 3-5
Scope statement in the design document

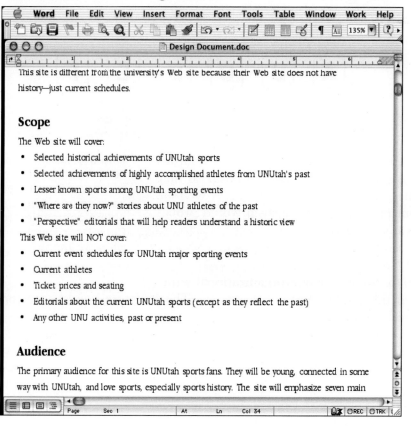

STEP-BY-STEP 3.4 Continued

2. Share all of the additions to your design document with a classmate or with your team. Have them decide whether your scope statement explains what your audience knows and what the Web site should cover.

3. Rewrite your paragraphs as needed and save them to the design document you've been working on in the previous Step-by-Steps. Leave your design document open for a later Step-by-Step.

How Should the Message Be Structured?

To fulfill the purpose and meet the needs of the audience you've just defined, your message must be organized in some way. Organization can come in many flavors, depending on what you are trying to accomplish. We need to take your message (the information on your Web site) and, based on what you know about your purpose and audience, organize it in preparation for turning it into a Web site.

Linear Structure

The simplest way to organize pages is in a *linear structure*. A linear organization works best when you want your user to see one page at a time and then move on, like reading a book or explaining a step-by-step process. Linear structure is also used when you don't want to give away the end of your story before you have finished it—as in a joke or a comic strip! Figure 3-6 shows a diagram of a linear structure.

FIGURE 3-6
Diagram of a linear structure

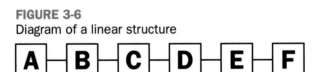

Stories, comic strips, and jokes all share this structure—they are linear: You step through them one step or page at a time, often for dramatic or humorous effect. Also, instructional sites are often linear so they can explain one step of the process at a time. A Web site instructing someone how to make sushi would probably have a linear structure.

Random Access Structure

Following are three common organizational structures. Each has advantages and disadvantages. The structure you choose for your Web site should mesh with your purpose.

Another way to organize information is by using *random access structure*. Random access lets you jump from one part of the site to any other page. Random access sites work best when you want your user to have quick access to all the information with a single mouse-click (see Figure 3-7).

FIGURE 3-7
Diagram of a random access structure

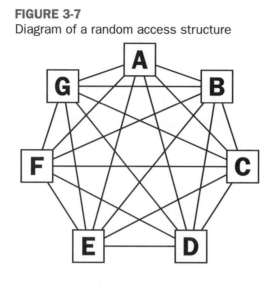

Random access structure can be very confusing if there is a large amount of information. But if you have a limited number of pages (say five or six), it is a good way to let your visitors get to all of them easily. If there are two pages, each page has one link. If there are three pages, each page would have to have two links (for a total of six links). If there were five pages, each page would have to have four links to the others (for a total of 20 links). The total number of links on a random access site is the total number of pages minus one times the number of pages: (Pages − 1) × Pages.

Net Fun

To see an example of a random access site visit *www.course.com* and locate the online companion for this book. Click on **Door Number 2** to get a feel for this popular Web structure.

For example, if there aren't too many places that sell sushi in your town, the random-access structure may be a good way to organize the sushi restaurant directory so that your audience can move from one link to the other quickly. (If there are more than seven sushi restaurants, a hierarchical Web site might be a better choice.)

Hierarchical Structure

Another very common structure is the *hierarchical structure*. Basically, a hierarchy looks like a family tree with parents and children (and sometimes grandchildren), as shown in Figure 3-8.

FIGURE 3-8
Diagram of a hierarchical structure

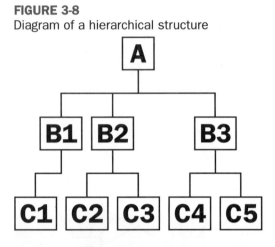

Hierarchies are a good way to organize information. They use categories and subcategories—something like what your English instructor taught you to do with an outline. Hierarchical structure is the most popular form of information organization for Web sites, especially large corporate Web sites.

Our university sports history site might be organized as a hierarchy, with the top category introducing the site and linking to pages about each individual sport. From the individual sports pages, links could be created to stories about the achievements of the teams and individuals in those sports.

Net Fun

Door Number 3 in the online companion Web site for this book will let you see a classic site using a hierarchical strategy.

Mixed Structure

Unfortunately, information does not always fit into such neat, clean structures. With some sites, some of your information should be organized one way and some in another. Sometimes you need a site that is partly random access, somewhat linear, and at times hierarchical, as shown in Figure 3-9. This is known as a mixed structure. Imagine the sushi site having a "how to" section about making sushi, a directory of local restaurants, and a general glossary of types of fish that are made into sushi. The "how to" section might be linear, the directory random access, and the glossary hierarchical—all in one site!

FIGURE 3-9
Diagram of a mixed structure

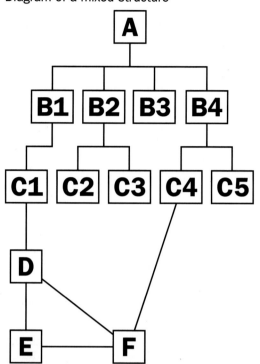

Organizing Your Message

To turn your message into any structure, you must first break your message up into smaller pieces of information we call *chunks*. This breaking of information into chunks will give you the building blocks of your structure—what you're going to put in those little boxes on your diagram.

Let's examine the University of Northern Utah sports Web site we have started. One way you could break up the information on your site would be by sports. Each sport would be a chunk. Then, you could break up each sport by the year. The years become a second level of chunking. Or, let's say that your Web site's audience is going to be most interested in the five most noteworthy athletes of UNU. In this case the athletes' names form the chunks of information. Another way you might break up the information is by date, making a history of UNU sports. In any case, the idea is to break the message up into the parts of which it is made. Remember, the purpose of breaking this information up is to make it fill your audience's needs—that is the key to deciding what kinds of chunks you will create.

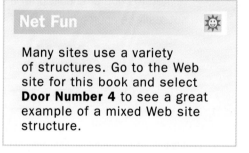

Net Fun

Many sites use a variety of structures. Go to the Web site for this book and select **Door Number 4** to see a great example of a mixed Web site structure.

The kind of chunks you choose can help you decide your Web site's structure. For example, if you chunk by sport and then by year, you have just started creating the chunks that would be perfect in a hierarchical structure. If you chunk by five outstanding athletes, they would fit nicely in a random access structure (because you've limited the chunks to just a handful of athletes). If you chunked the information into historical chunks, they could be structured linearly into a history, year by year.

STEP-BY-STEP 3.5

1. On a piece of paper, write your main topic in the middle of the paper, like: "university sports history," "old books," or "what kinds of fish can be used for sushi?" With your classmates, brainstorm about chunks of information related to this topic and write them down around the message statement. Figure 3-10 is an example of how it might look.

FIGURE 3-10
Results of brainstorming with chunked information

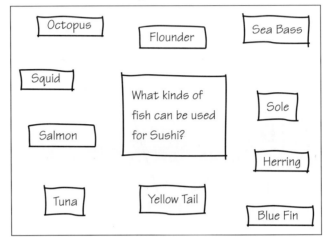

2. Look over the chunks you've written down. Do you think you might have missed any? Have you accidentally duplicated some? Are there chunks that don't belong at all? Can any of the chunks be grouped topically under one of the other chunks?

3. On your paper, draw a line from each chunk to the message statement, or if a chunk is more closely related to another chunk, draw a line between them (see Figure 3-11). Delete any chucks that may not really be appropriate to this site.

FIGURE 3-11
Chunked information with lines showing some relationships

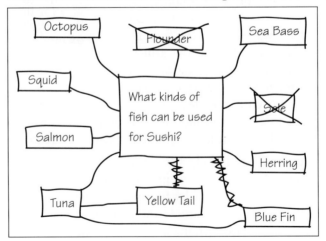

STEP-BY-STEP 3.5 Continued

4. Look carefully at your paper. Some kind of structure should begin to emerge. (You may need to cross out some of the lines you have drawn, and draw others to make the structure clear.)

5. Redraw your chart, being careful to note how things are related so you can draw it more neatly. Draw boxes around the chunks and lines between the boxes to show relationships. You may need to repeat this exercise a few times before the chart is clear—like the one in Figure 3-12. Review the different structures we discussed above if you're not clear on how to organize your chunks.

FIGURE 3-12
Chunked information rearranged in a hierarchical structure

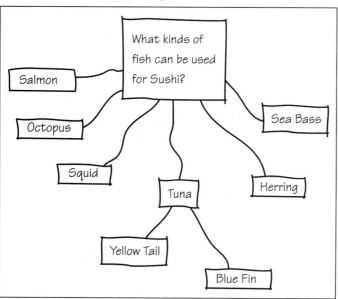

What you have just finished is called a *flowchart*. (Notice that the flowchart in the illustration is the beginning of a hierarchical organization because some of the chunks have "sub-chunks") A flowchart illustrates how the information in a Web site (or any other kind of document, for that matter) flows—how the information relates to one another. Your flowchart will help you see and understand at one glance how your information is put together. It is a valuable addition to your design document.

STEP-BY-STEP 3.6

1. Using drawing software, re-create your flowchart as a picture or as a graphic using one of the four Web site structures identified in this chapter: random, linear, hierarchical, or mixed.

2. Insert your diagram into your design document under the heading **Structure—Flowchart** (just before the Resource List).

3. Resave your design document and print out a copy

4. Close all open applications.

> ### Extra Challenge
>
> A flowchart is a snapshot of the information on your Web site; that is, it shows at a glance how the information on your site is organized. Are there any other ways you can use flowcharts to represent information? What kind of flowchart might you use to show a snapshot of your audience or of your purpose?

Design Document Outline

You've been building the design document by inserting things according to our discussion, not in the order they will appear. If you have been following the Step-by-Step activities closely, you should now have a design document whose outline looks similar to this:

A. Message

B. Scope

C. Audience

D. Audience Background

E. Persona

F. Purpose

G. Structure—Flowchart

H. Resource List

Technically, "Scope" is part of "Message" and "Audience Background" and "Persona" are part of "Audience." So you could modify your headings to show these relationships, if you wanted:

1. Message

    a. Scope

2. Audience

    a. Audience Background

    b. Persona

3. Purpose

4. Structure—Flowchart

5. Resource List

SUMMARY

In this lesson, you learned:

- To identify and document your Web site's message.

- To identify your audience so that you can tailor the information contained within your Web site to the audience's needs.

- To identify, develop, and document your Web site's purpose and scope.

- That using a flowchart allows you to structure your Web site's information.

VOCABULARY *Review*

Define the following terms:

Chunks	Information design	Persona
Design document	Linear structure	Random access structure
Flowchart	Mixed structure	Scope statement
Hierarchical structure		

REVIEW *Questions*

TRUE/FALSE

Circle T if the statement is true or F if the statement is false

T   F   1. Knowing your audience is part of information design.

T   F   2. A flowchart will help you understand your purpose better.

T   F   3. A hierarchical structure is especially good for stories.

T   F   4. A random access structure will help you organize lots of information.

T   F   5. A persona can help you focus on your audience

WRITTEN QUESTIONS

Write a brief answer to each of the following questions.

1. What kinds of Web sites would benefit from a random access structure? Give a specific example.

2. What kinds of Web sites would benefit from a linear structure? Give a specific example.

3. What kinds of Web sites would benefit from a hierarchical structure? Give a specific example.

4. What kinds of Web sites would benefit from a mixed structure? Give a specific example.

PROJECTS

PROJECT 3-1

Wally Woodword owns a small cabinet-making business. He creates kitchen and bathroom cabinets and custom wood furnishings for homes. His buyers are homeowners. He uses a variety of woods for his projects including oak, pine, birch, maple, poplar, mahogany, and cherry. He wants to sell more cabinets.

Wally feels that if he can create a Web site, he can reach more homeowners. He has asked you to come up with the information design for his new site. Create a short design document for his site. Be creative! If you can impress Wally with your ideas, you may get the job of designing his Web site. Include the following elements:

- Message statement
- Audience statement
- Purpose statement
- Audience background statement
- Scope
  - This Web site will cover . . .
  - This Web site will not cover . . .
- Flowchart

TEAMWORK PROJECT

Wally Woodword's Wood Works, Inc., faces a great deal of competition. Wally is wondering several things:

1. What other cabinetmakers have Web sites?

2. What online resources are available about cabinet making?

3. What information is available about various kinds of wood used in woodworking (oak, pine, birch, maple, poplar, mahogany, and cherry)?

Wally wants a resource list that includes resources on each of these topics. Searching all of this information on the Web might be difficult for one person, but if you divide up the task between three or more team members, it will be a snap!

As a team, prepare a research list for Wally on each of these three topics.

CRITICAL*Thinking*

Having created two design documents, you now understand a great deal about the basics of information design. You have learned how to define the audience, purpose, and message of a Web site. With what you know about design to this point, write a 100-word answer to one or more of the inquiries below.

ACTIVITY 3-1

Based on what you have learned so far, which element of information design do you feel is the most important to define: the audience, the purpose, or the message? Explain your answer.

ACTIVITY 3-2

Explain how the three elements of audience, purpose, and message work together to help organize a great Web site.

ACTIVITY 3-3

Why is it helpful to define the scope of your Web site?

INTERACTION DESIGN

OBJECTIVES

Upon completion of this lesson, you should be able to:

- Create a storyboard that represents the information available on your Web site.

- Identify the welcome page of your Web site.

- Show your visitors where they are while navigating your site.

- Decide how your visitors will move around your site.

- Use context devices to organize the user interface for your Web site.

- Test your Web site's content and navigation.

Estimated Time: 2.5 hours

VOCABULARY

Background

Banner

Context device

Focus group

Heading

Interaction design

Navigation bar

Path

Storyboard

Wayfinding

Welcome page

Two Elements of Interaction Design

Interaction design is concerned with two things: how visitors to your Web site will find their way around (navigation) and how they will play with the material on your Web site (interaction).

In the last lesson, you were able to figure out how your information should be put together (organized). This organization is usually the basis of how your Web site can be built to make it easy to get around with a minimum of hassle. That is navigation. Take a look at *yahoo.com* or *snap.com* for good examples of navigation.

If your Web site visitors are *doing* something with your information, they are more likely to remember what you have to say. Interactivity is what visitors can *do* with your information. Navigation and interactivity, if done right, will help your audience understand and remember your message. *Disney.go.com* and *macromedia.com* offer good examples of interaction.

To make all of this work, designers will often use a couple of tricks of the trade. One is a tool called a storyboard, and the other is a set of building blocks called context devices. In the following sections, you will learn more about both of these.

A Designer Tool: The Storyboard

Sometimes engineers will create models to decide whether something they are trying to build is going to work. This gives them the opportunity to visualize and to test scale models before they build the life-sized items. Web designers use a similar tool called a *storyboard*. Storyboards are a technique developed by Walt Disney to help animators make cartoons. Before they would actually begin the meticulous work of drawing individual cells, animators would work out the overall storyline, the scenery (backgrounds), and the general

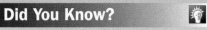

Did You Know?

Storyboards are often arranged on corkboards using pins or tacks, or they are placed on magnetic boards with magnets to make the contents easy to move around as needed. Storyboarding software is also available.

concepts from which they would all work to create the cartoon. As it turns out, storyboards are also a perfect tool for planning Web sites.

If you made a flowchart in the last lesson, making a storyboard will be very simple. It's made up of cards or pieces of paper on which you write ideas. These cards can then be organized, moved about, added to, or taken away until you are comfortable with their arrangement. You can use the cards to represent whole Web pages or parts of a single Web page. In this exercise, we'll use each card to represent a page on your Web site.

S TEP-BY-STEP 4.1

1. Get a number of blank 3×5 index cards, or cut pieces of blank paper to approximately that size.

2. Open your design document and turn to the flowchart you created in Step-by-Step 3.6.

3. Each box on your flowchart should have a name or a title written inside that represents a chunk of information that you have defined (see Figure 3-12 in Lesson 3). Copy the words from the boxes on your flowchart to the top of your 3×5 cards. Use one card for each box on your flowchart. Leave plenty of room on the cards—you'll be writing lots more on them. Each one of these will represent a page of your Web site. (See Figure 4-1 for an example.)

FIGURE 4-1
A storyboard card

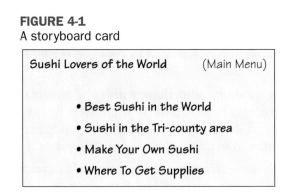

STEP-BY-STEP 4.1 Continued

4. Arrange the 3×5 cards in the same pattern as the top-ics or "chunks" of information appearing on your flow-chart. You can place the cards on a piece of poster board, on a white board, or on a blank wall using small pieces of tape on the back of each card to hold it in place—but don't tape the cards securely. You want to be able to move them around and take them down to write on them. If available, a bulletin board or a mag-netic board would also work well. (See Figure 4-2 for an example of the arrangement of 3×5 cards.)

FIGURE 4-2
A storyboard

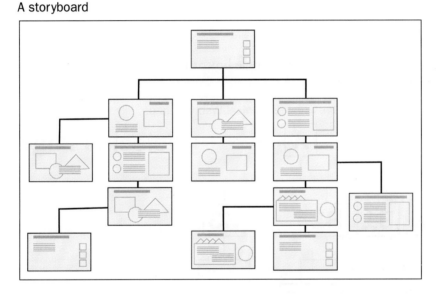

Context Devices

Context Device #1: Start at the Beginning

Books have title pages; newspapers have banners; TV shows have opening credits. Nearly every media type has something to let you know that you're at the beginning. The Web is no different.

The front page of every newspaper (and a lot of Web sites) has a ***banner*** that stretches across the top, identifying the paper. Famous banners like *The Wall Street Journal* and the *San Francisco Chronicle* are classic examples. Similarly, books have title pages that tell you the title of the book, the author, and the publisher. Television programs have opening credits that tell you the name of the show. Banners, title pages, and opening credits are all starting devices that tell you that you're looking at the beginning of something—at the starting point. Similarly, Web sites require a way to let viewers know that they are at the beginning of the Web site. This is often accomplished with a ***welcome page.***

The welcome page may include an index or a table of contents. It is here that visitors will determine if your site is what they are looking for, and it is from here that they will go to see the rest of your Web site.

As you examined the different kinds of structures in Lesson 3, did you notice that some of them have a natural starting point?

In the case of a linear structure, it's the one on the left—the "first page" (See Figure 4-3).

FIGURE 4-3
The welcome page in a linear Web site is the first page

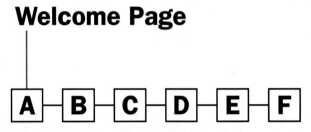

In the hierarchical structure, it's the single box at the top (see Figure 4-4).

FIGURE 4-4
The welcome page in a hierarchical Web site is usually the top page

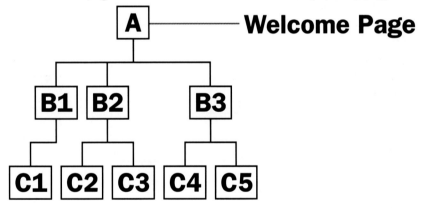

In the random access structure, any page can be the starting point because all the pages lead to all the others. But usually, there's one that is at the "center" of things and can be designated as the starting point for the rest (see Figure 4-5). Because this is just a sampling of structures, you may have a structure that doesn't follow these formats, but there is almost always a starting point. If there doesn't seem to be any one page that would serve as a starting point, you may need to create a welcome page with links to all of the other pages.

FIGURE 4-5
A random access Web site may have a center page which may be the welcome page

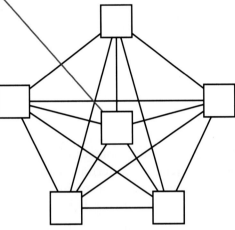

Welcome Page

STEP-BY-STEP 4.2

1. Identify your welcome page. Which card do you think would make the best starting point for your Web site's visitors? Write WP (for welcome page) in the top right corner of the card that will represent your starting point on your storyboard. (In some structures—such as random access—you may need to create and add a new card as your welcome page.)

Extra Challenge

What is the starting device for a movie? What is the starting device for a magazine? What is the starting device for a class period or a business meeting? What is the starting device for a trial in a court of law?

2. Start designing your welcome page. Pull your welcome page card (with the WP) from your storyboard and start sketching a rough outline of what you want your welcome page to look like. Use a pencil and write lightly so you can sketch, erase, and sketch again. Make sure the title of your site is written at or near the top. The title can become your banner if you plan it as such.

3. Plan how your banner will look on your welcome page. Will it be all text or will it include a graphic or an image with multimedia effects? If you make a mistake or change your mind, create a new card.

4. Place your welcome page back on your storyboard.

STEP-BY-STEP 4.2 Continued

5. Open your design document, and write the heading **Welcome Page**, and add a one-paragraph description (about 75 words) as to the purpose and content of this important page. This page will appear as the last thing just before the references. Following is an example.

   Welcome Page

   The banner for this page will read, Fish Used for Sushi. The page will welcome the visitor to the Web site, explain the purpose of the site in a short paragraph, and list several links to the various kinds of fish that can be used to prepare sushi.

6. If you are talented with graphics software, draw a sample of what your welcome page may look like and copy it into your design document under the description you just prepared.

7. Save your design document and leave it open for the next Step-by-Step.

Four More Context Devices: Where Are We?

Have you ever noticed that you can tell when a television commercial is coming on? Why is that? TV broadcast stations use various *context devices* to tell you what show you're looking at and that a commercial is coming. Sometimes they cut or fade to a black screen. Other times there is a short title sequence (check out reruns of *Star Trek* for an example.) You may not even notice these devices, but without them, you might start to confuse the program with the commercials (something the sponsors would probably love but the television producers would not).

Newspapers, books, and magazines also use context devices to help you tell where you are and where you can go next. Headings, headlines, page numbers, and columns guide you through books and newspapers and help you understand the context of what you are reading. Not surprisingly then, Web pages use some obvious context devices too. Following are a few of them:

- A *banner* is a graphic across the top or side that tells users what Web site it is (like the banner on a newspaper that tells you you're looking at the front page of the *Chicago Tribune*).

- A *heading* is a one- to eight-word description in bold or large type above a block of content. Headings are used to describe portions of the content (such as chapter titles and subheadings in a book). Look at the phrase "Four More Context Devices: Where Are We?" above. That is a heading.

- *Backgrounds* are visual cues that lie underneath the content of the page that tell users what Web site this Web page is part of. This type of context device can be subtle and understated. It is usually part of how the page looks, but can include a common graphic that is found on each page.

- *Navigation bars* appear on each page of the Web site. Usually these have a unique "look" that helps users tell they are still in the same Web site—while also enabling them to see where they are (what page they are on).

- Sometimes the *content* itself, that is the *pictures* and *text* that make up the message of your Web site, act as context devices. They do this by having a particular "look" to them that helps the visitor recognize that they are still in a particular Web site. For example, if all of the pictures are a certain style of cartoons with a particular color scheme, when visitors see those cartoons with that color scheme they will immediately recognize where they are.

STEP-BY-STEP 4.3

1. Look at Figure 4-6. Can you identify all of the possible context devices on this page? Name at least three of them. (Read the Communication Skills special feature on the next page to see if your answers are correct.)

FIGURE 4-6
A Corporate View communications page using several context devices

2. From your storyboard select a page other than the welcome page. We will call this a content card. All the cards on your storyboard other than your welcome page card are content cards.

3. On a new index card, sketch out a rough idea of what you think a typical content card should look like. Block out squares where you intend to display text, and make sketches where you think graphics will go.

4. Then, on the same card, define two context devices. For example, one may be a picture found on each page. Another may be a consistent color on each Web page site. A third might be a "Return to Welcome Page" button or a navigation bar that can be found on every page. Don't be too fastidious (careful) about how it looks. This is just a rough sketch, not a finished product. (If it takes you more than about ten minutes to create this first card, it's too detailed.)

5. Create two additional variations of the same page. Take two new index cards and sketch different designs on them, each a variation of your page ideas. Organize the content differently on each card.

6. Share your three sketches with a partner (if you're a member of a design team, share them with your team). With his or her help, decide which of the sketches is the best one for your content.

7. Sketch the winning design on the content card and place it back on your storyboard.

8. Each of your cards, which will later be developed into Web pages, requires the same context devices. Quickly sketch your context devices on each of the cards on your storyboard.

STEP-BY-STEP 4.3 Continued

9. Go to your design document and defend your choice of design and context devices. Why did you choose the context and navigation aids you sketched in this activity? Enter the words **Context Devices** and write a short paragraph (under 100 words) describing the context and navigation devices you have selected and why you find them effective. Place this at the end of your document, just before the references. A partial example is given below.

Context Devices

I chose a navigation bar, a common background color scheme, and links back to the welcome page as my navigation and context devices because . . . .

10. If you are talented with graphics software, draw a sample of what your context devices may look like and copy it into your design document under the description you just wrote.

11. Save your design document and leave it open for the next Step-by-Step.

> ### Extra Challenge
>
> Are there any context devices that help people as they drive down the road and navigate through traffic jams? What technologies have been created to provide a safe context for motorists? How do these devices help prevent accidents?

Communication Skills

You were asked to identify the context devices on the Web page shown in Figure 4-6. There are at least six. A color bar on the left side of the window uses the same color on all similar Web pages. Inside that color bar is a list of links that are consistent throughout the site. The Corporate Communication banner appears on top of every page in the section. The Corporate View logo in the top left corner also appears on all pages and is hyperlinked back to the welcome page. Headings are used to identify and separate different topics. And, finally, the hypertext links help visitors access other important parts of this site.

Refining Your Navigation

When you are in an unfamiliar building, such as a museum, library, or large shopping mall, you will often find a large map containing the words "You Are Here" with an arrow pointing to a spot on the map, as shown in Figure 4-7. This map provides you with the two elements of good navigation: It tells you where you are right now, and it shows you how to get around—where other things are in relation to where you are.

FIGURE 4-7
A typical building map

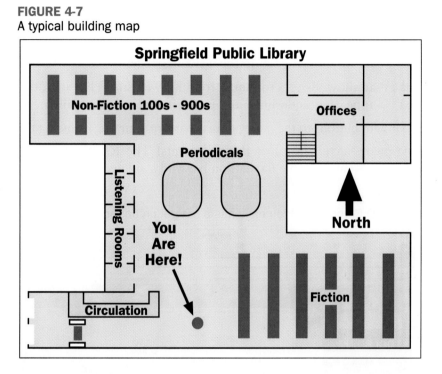

That is what good navigation in a Web site should do as well. It should show you:

■ Where you are right now.

■ Where you can go.

If you think about it, you'll see that these two are closely related. How can you tell where you want to go if you don't know where you are right now? How can you tell where you are right now, if you can't see any other landmarks?

Where Are You Going?

The Web browser buttons along the top of the browser window help make Web page navigation easy. They allow your audience members to "back out" of a page or to "go home" to where they started if they get lost. However, the surest sign of amateur design is if the visitors get lost in the Web site and need to use the "back" or "home" buttons to get "unlost." There are many ways that a visitor can navigate your site, and it starts on your welcome page.

A welcome page can be like a title page, or it can be like a table of contents. A title page explains what the site is about and displays banners and pictures that will attract visitors to delve deeper into your Web site. A table of contents is simply a list of places your visitor can go. Just as a table of contents in a book tells you exactly what page to go to for specific information, you can move directly to the desired Web page by clicking on a link.

Your welcome page should combine *both* a title page *and* a table of contents. Your welcome page can include:

■ A list of links to the other pages.

■ Hyperlinked pictures scattered on the page.

■ A navigation bar with buttons to the most popular or important parts of your site.

■ Clickable areas (text, graphics, or buttons) to take users elsewhere, usually to navigate the site.

After you have decided how your users will move from your welcome page to your content pages, you need to find a way to allow them to move back to the starting point or to move ahead to other Web pages. There are many ways to do this, including the use of the following elements:

■ A button or link as a way to get back to the welcome page.

■ Hypertext links that allow visitors to jump around a Web site. They look different from the rest of the text by appearing underlined and in a different color, usually in blue or purple.

■ A navigation bar with buttons to the most popular parts of your site, including the welcome page.

Some welcome pages have several of these elements! The RAND Corporation's welcome page shown in Figure 4-8 has a simple navigation bar and a sidebar list of links.

FIGURE 4-8
The RAND Corporation Web page has a navigation bar and a sidebar list

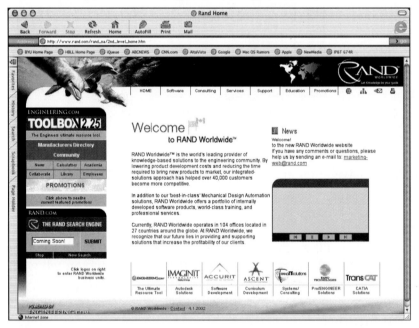

Linear structures often don't have a menu or table of contents (though, like a book, they can). In a linear structure, the navigation control is often three simple buttons: one to take you to the next Web page, one to take you back to the previous Web page, and one to take you to the welcome page, each in a single click (see Figure 4-9).

FIGURE 4-9
Navigation controls for a linear structure

STEP-BY-STEP 4.4

1. Open your browser and key **www.course.com** in the address box. Once the Course Technology Web site has opened, use the Search box to perform a search using the title of this book or its ISBN number. Information about this book will appear in the Search Results.

2. Click the title of this book.

3. In the page that appears, click **Download Student Files**, and then click **Web Design Basics** under the Student Online Companion heading.

> **Net Tip**
>
> Make a list of the wonderful sites you see on the Web. Keep this list in an appendix of your design document for future reference, or create a Favorites List folder and bookmark your favorites in your Web browser. These can be a source of inspiration for your own Web sites.

4. Click **Door Number 5**. Look at the welcoming Web page that appears. Answer these questions (ask your instructor what form your answers should take):
   - What things make it clear that this is a welcoming Web page?
   - Can you tell what the entire site is going to be about?
   - What clues have they given you to help you decide where to go next?
   - Which of these navigation elements could you use in your welcome page?

5. Click the Back button and then click **Door Number 6** and analyze the site that appears. Answer these questions about this site:
   - How do you know that this is a welcome page?
   - Can you tell what the entire site is going to be about?
   - What clues have they given you to help you decide where to go next?
   - Which of these navigation elements could you use in your welcome page?

6. Close your browser.

7. Given the structure and content of your site, select a navigation method that you would like to use. You can use a navigation bar, a table of contents, or hyperlinks.

Communication Skills

QUESTIONS, QUESTIONS

In Lesson 3 you identified several questions that helped you create the initial design document. Here are some questions to help you with this lesson:

- What would work best to show your users the way?

- How will they find their way around the site? How will they know where they are in the structure of the site?

- Is there a graphic or metaphor that would help them understand the information in the site better?

- How can you make the site easier or more fun to use?

STEP-BY-STEP 4.4 Continued

8. On your welcome page card sketch the method you will use to move your visitors from your welcome page to other information, content, or Web pages on the site. Remember, you can use a new card to redraw the welcome page if you need to.

9. Given the structure and content of your site, select a way to get from your content pages back to your welcome page and elsewhere on your site. In a linear structure or random access structure, this may be a single button or link. In a hierarchical structure it may involve steps to navigate back up the hierarchy to the home page.

10. Write or sketch the method you select on one card on your storyboard. If you decide to use a button bar, define each button and explain where each button will take your visitor.

11. Share your navigation methods with a partner, or, if you are working as a team, with your team members. Discuss whether the methods chosen for navigation are best suited to your Web site, and make changes as necessary.

12. When you have finalized both methods (how to move from your welcome page and how to move back) add these methods to all of your content cards. Remember, you can use new index cards to redraw your content cards if you need to.

13. Go to your design document and explain your navigation system. Why did you choose the navigation aids you sketched in this activity? Enter the words **Navigation and Interaction** and write a short paragraph (under 100 words) describing the context and navigation devices you have selected and why you find them effective. This should appear just before the references at the end of your design document. A partial example is given below.

> ### Extra Challenge
>
> Go back and read the message, audience, scope, and purpose statements you wrote in Lesson 3. Which navigation system will best meet your audience's needs? Could your navigation system be improved to accomplish your purpose in communicating your message more clearly to your audience?

Navigation and Interaction

I chose a navigation bar, which serves as both a context device and an interactive navigation tool. I also have a picture that will appear on each page that, if clicked on, will take the visitor back to my welcome page. Interactivity is enhanced by . . . .

14. If you are skilled with graphics software, draw a sample of what your navigation tools may look like and copy them into your design document under the description you just prepared.

15. Save your design document and leave it open for the next Step-by-Step.

Knowing Where You Are

Now that your visitors know how to find their way from one place to the next, you need to give them clues as to where they are right now. This is sometimes called *wayfinding*. Techniques for wayfinding in your Web site also differ depending on the structure of the site. In a story or another linear structure, you may have a page number on each page. Having the page number prominently displayed, as shown in Figure 4-10, will help your viewers know where they are.

FIGURE 4-10
The structure of a linear Web site

You can also add the total number of pages, for example "page 3 of 12." This method not only tells visitors where they are (page 3), it also tells them where they are in relation to the whole story or sequence of pages (about a fourth of the way through). An example of this can be seen in Figure 4-11.

FIGURE 4-11
A Web site with page numbers in the form "page x of y"

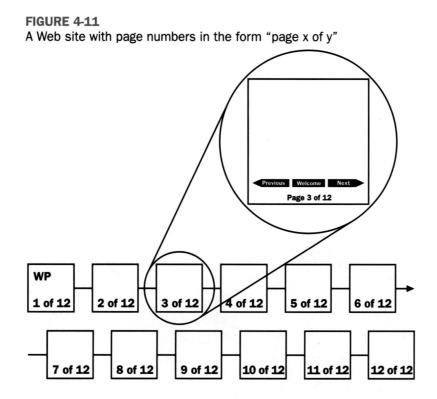

In a Web site based upon a random access structure, it is a little more difficult to keep track of your location since you can basically get from anywhere to anywhere. In this case, a simple page title is usually enough, providing that the links to the other pages use the same titles (see Figure 4-12). You could also use an illustration, a picture, or a graphical icon.

FIGURE 4-12
A random access Web page with titles

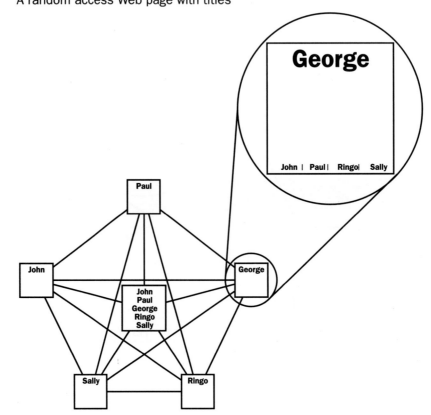

One of the most common Web structures is the hierarchical structure. It can also be one of the most complicated for wayfinding. However, a simple method called a *path* can be used to show viewers where they are. Figure 4-13 shows how the movement down a hierarchy is translated into a path. In this case, the user has navigated from the "Animals" page through the "Horses" and "Racehorses" categories to a page about "Standard-bred" horses. A common way to show this is to separate the items in the path with some kind of punctuation (in this case, a line break, some spaces, and an arrow) to show what path was traveled to get to where the user is now. This path may appear at the top of the page as part of a navigation bar, at the bottom of the page, or even in the contents of the page. To see a good example of a path, check out *www.yahoo.com*. Just under the heading is a path.

FIGURE 4-13
The path from the general term "Animals" to the specific term "Standard-bred" racehorses

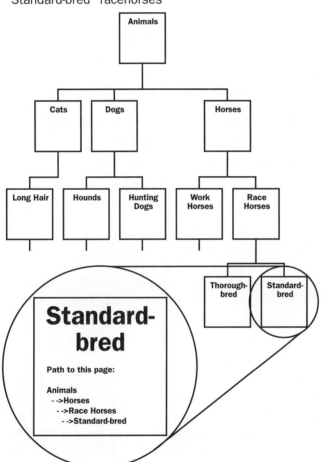

STEP-BY-STEP 4.5

1. Given the structure and content of your site, select a method to show your viewers where they are in your Web site. You may use one of the techniques above or make up your own. Sketch your ideas on one of your content cards.

2. Share your ideas for wayfinding with a partner or with your team. Make corrections to your idea as necessary.

3. Sketch the basics of your wayfinding method onto all of your cards. Remember, you can redraw and replace cards on your storyboard if you need to.

Extra Challenge

Once again, out on the open road in your car ... are there any wayfinding devices that can help you find your way? In construction zones, are there any context devices that help drivers make decisions about where they are and where they need to go?

4. Write a brief description of how you are going to help visitors through wayfinding. Add this description in your design document. Enter the word **Wayfinding** and write a short paragraph (under 100 words) describing your place-finding strategy. Insert this before the Resource List in your design document.

5. Draw a picture of your solution and include it in your design document after your paragraph. Or, if you are skilled with graphics software, draw a sample of what your wayfinding tools may look like and copy them into your design document under the description you just prepared.

6. Save your design document and leave it open for the next Step-by-Step.

Testing Your Design

Testing? Test what? Test your design, that's what. Just because you haven't created your Web pages yet doesn't mean that you have nothing to test. You can test your design to make sure that it is complete. You can use the storyboard to test whether it is easy to use.

Does It Have Everything?

There are several ways to test for completeness, but one of the easiest is to show the design, including the design document and storyboard, to an expert. For example, if your Web site is about making sushi, you probably want to speak to a sushi chef. Explain to the expert who your audience is, what your target scope is, and what you're hoping the users of your Web site will learn. You can ask the expert a series of questions. The answers will tell you things you may need to change.

OK. That's all well and good. But what if an expert on your chosen subject isn't available? Never fear; having *anyone* look at your design is better than nothing. You may not be able to find an exact match in the form of an expert, but maybe you can find something close. For example, if there are no sushi chefs in your area to evaluate your sushi Web site, how about any kind of chef? Maybe a butcher at a local grocery store with experience in preparing fish would do. You get the idea.

STEP-BY-STEP 4.6

1. Brainstorm for a list of people who would be considered experts in what your Web site is about. Write the list down, and next to each name, briefly describe each person's specific expertise.

2. Prioritize your list according to who would be the best expert with whom to consult. Do this by putting a number 1 next to the best choice, number 2 next to the second best, and so forth. An example is shown in Figure 4-14.

FIGURE 4-14
A list of possible experts you could consult with on a site about sushi, numbered according to their expertise

1.	Masa Tanaka	Sushi chef at the House of Sushi
2.	Fred Holsigner	Amateur sushi chef (friend)
3.	Marsha Takanaga	Works at Fish Market and is an amateur Japanese cook
4.	Don Paxman	Fish chef at the Café Ritz
5.	Deborah Davis	Butcher at Decker Grocery—knows a lot about cuts of fish
6.	Jerry Broadbent	Lived in Japan and knows about kinds of sushi
7.	Louise Bray	Sushi lover

3. Starting with number 1 on your list, try to contact that person to see if he or she would be willing to look at your design to see if it is complete. Continue down the list until you've found someone who can help you.

4. Meet with your expert and show him or her the materials. Explain how the site will work when finished and ask if you've left anything out. Your questions may include some of these:

   ■ Have I covered the subject well enough for my audience?

   ■ Have I left anything out?

   ■ Is there anything here that I should leave out?

   ■ Do you have any other concerns about what I've shown you?

5. Carefully take notes on his or her answers. You will use this material to make changes to your design.

6. Now that you have some ideas on whether you have covered your material completely, you will want to make adjustments to your design. This may include modifying any of the defining statements in the design document (audience, purpose, or message, among others) or adding or taking away cards from your storyboard. Make those changes now and then save your design document, if necessary.

Is It Easy to Use?

Does it take an expert to know whether your site is easy to navigate? Nope. Everyday users of your Web site are the best judges of whether your site is easy to get around in. To test this, you put together what is called a focus group. A *focus group* is nothing more than a few people (three to six) from your target audience. You show them the design and ask what they think. You prepare for a focus group session by deciding how you will present the design and what questions you will ask.

Unfortunately, you may not find members of your specific audience close by. For example, if your Web site is for lovers of country music, you may have no friends or acquaintances who like country music. If this happens use people who are like your audience in other ways—for example, they may like other kinds of music. It's more important that they can be good judges of whether the site is easy to navigate. If all else fails, use classmates as focus group members—any focus group is better than none. After all, people are more alike than different!

STEP-BY-STEP 4.7

1. Identify a number of people (between three and six) who might be willing to serve as your focus group. Contact these people and ask them to join you at a specified time and place. If you are doing this as a class activity, you will need to arrange to be on other learners' focus groups so they can be on yours.

2. Organize your material to present to the focus group. Generally, you will tell them why you have asked them to assemble (to review the Web site to make sure it will be easy to use) and the purpose, audience, and message of the site. Then, using the storyboard, walk them through how a typical user would view and navigate the Web site.

3. Also prepare a number of questions regarding navigating your site that you would like them to answer. Following are some ideas for questions:
   - Is this a good way to organize this material? If not, what would be a better way to organize it?
   - Is this the best structure (linear, random access, hierarchical, or other) for this material?
   - Is it easy and obvious how to get from [one place in your Web site] to [another place in your Web site]? (use specific pages)

4. Conduct your focus group session with the approach you prepared in steps 2 and 3. The total time should be one-half hour or less.

5. Carefully take notes on the answers provided by your focus group members. You will use this information to make changes to your design. (You may find it easier to tape record or videotape the session and then take notes later. This will allow you to listen more carefully to what the focus group is saying and ensure that you don't miss anything. It will also allow you to spend more time talking with the group members and less time writing what they are saying.)

6. Now that you have some ideas on whether you have covered your material completely, you will want to make adjustments to your design. This may include modifying any of the defining statements in the design document (audience, purpose, or message, among others) or adding or taking away cards from your storyboard. Make those changes now. Your storyboard will now start to become more stable, so you can tape the cards down to the poster board, if you wish.

7. Save and close your design document and close the application in which it is written.

SUMMARY

In this lesson, you learned:

■ How to create a storyboard that represents the information of your Web site.

■ How to identify the welcome page of your Web site.

■ Ways to show your visitors where they are while navigating your site.

■ To determine how your visitors will move around your site.

■ To use context devices to organize the user interface for your Web site.

■ To test your Web site's content and navigation.

VOCABULARY *Review*

Define the following terms:

Background	Heading	Storyboard
Banner	Interaction design	Wayfinding
Context device	Navigation bar	Welcome page
Focus group	Path	

REVIEW *Questions*

TRUE/FALSE

Circle T if the statement is true or F if the statement is false.

T   F   1. For a Web site, a storyboard is an expanded flowchart.

T   F   2. A banner often tells you where you can go in the Web site.

T   F   3. A background can lie underneath the content of the Web site.

T   F   4. Good navigation tells you one thing: where you can go.

T   F   5. A path is a good navigation device for a linear structure.

FILL IN THE BLANK

Complete the following sentences by writing the correct word or words in the blanks provided.

1. Interaction design is concerned with two things, _____ and _____.
2. Wayfinding is a part of _____.
3. A good wayfinding device for a linear structure is a(n)_____.
4. A good wayfinding device for a hierarchical structure is a(n)_____.
5. You can test your interaction design for two things:_____ and _____.

WRITTEN QUESTIONS

Write a brief answer to each of the following questions.

1. Why are storyboards such powerful tools in Web page design?

2. What is the purpose of banners and why are they used frequently on Web sites?

3. Why are welcome pages needed; in other words, what purposes do they serve?

4. What is a context device? Explain these powerful tools with examples.

PROJECTS

PROJECT 4-1

Continuing to advise Wally Woodword's Wood Works, *Inc.* in the development of its Web site, you are asked to storyboard the cabinetmaker's Web site. (Review the Projects from Lesson 3.) Storyboard the site based on what you know about:

- Welcome pages
- Banners
- Context devices
- Navigation systems
- Wayfinders

Enter your new design ideas for Wally in the design document you started creating for the cabinetmaker in Lesson 3.

TEAMWORK PROJECT

Form a team of three or four people and search the Web looking for the best examples you can find of the following:

- Best welcome page
- Best banner
- Best navigation system
- Best wayfinding idea
- Most impressive context devices

Prepare a short presentation about each of your five selections. Present your choices to the other teams and explain why you selected the pages you did.

CRITICAL*Thinking*

With what you have learned about interaction design to this point, write a 100-word response to each of the activities below.

SCANS ACTIVITY 4-1

What is the most useful navigation system that you have seen? Why do you prefer this system to the other possible options?

SCANS ACTIVITY 4-2

Are wayfinding techniques really important? Explain your answer and include samples of good wayfinding techniques you have seen in your searching of the Web.

PRESENTATION DESIGN

Visualizing Your Web Site

Presentation design is sometimes called visual design. It is planning how your Web site will look. Some of the questions you need to ask to begin this planning process are:

- What colors will look good together on your site?
- What fonts or styles of type will you use for the written part of your Web pages?
- What graphics and multimedia effects are needed?
- How will all of these elements be combined or arranged into an attractive layout?

There have been many books written on the subject of graphic or presentation design. It's probably pretty obvious that the more you know about making good art, the better you will be at making your site look good. You may be surprised to learn, however, that the people who have the most to do with creating a "look" for a Web site are not artists—at least not in the traditional sense. These are not necessarily people who know how to paint or draw (though many have those talents as well). Rather, these are people who know how to put things together to make them look visually appealing. That is why they are often called graphic designers. In fact, when you say the word *design* or *designer*, most people think you are speaking of graphic design or a graphic designer.

Following are some tips and techniques that will help you decide on a visual "look" for your Web site as well as how to apply that "look."

An Artist's Tool: Thumbnail Sketches

Professional Web designers doodle. They draw lots of tiny little pictures to see what things are going to look like. Like a scientist doing little experiments, the graphic designer doodles these little pictures to test ideas and different looks. These little drawings help them think about the visual aspects of the Web pages they are designing. They make lots of these before settling on an idea. Like professionals, you can also use little sketches to help make choices about your Web site's presentation design.

One kind of little drawings that graphic designers make are called **thumbnail sketches** because they are very small (like your thumbnail—though they're not usually *that* small). These thumbnail sketches are similar to the sketches you made in the last chapter for your storyboard, but they serve a different purpose. The storyboard helped you get a handle on your Web site's interaction; thumbnails help you focus on how your Web pages will actually look. The two may be similar—or completely different!

To do a sketch, you need to get rid of details so you can get the overall picture quickly. One way to get rid of some of the detail is to use **greeking**, which is substituting straight or squiggly lines for text. Though you will probably want to go ahead and write out the headings, you can use heavier lines for larger or bold text, and lighter lines for smaller or lighter text. Greeking can give you the "look" of text in your thumbnail sketch without taking the time to write it all out. Figure 5-1 is a thumbnail sketch of the Web page shown in Figure 5-2.

FIGURE 5-1
A thumbnail sketch of the Southern Virginia University Web page

FIGURE 5-2
The actual Web page for Southern Virginia University

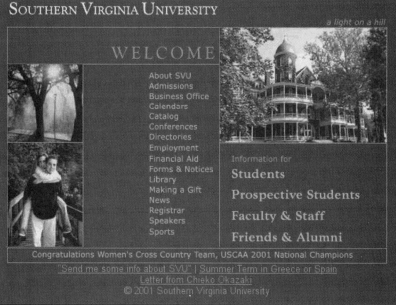

A typical size for a thumbnail sketch of a screen is no more than a couple of inches wide by an inch or so tall, though they can be larger if need be. One of the tricks to making thumbnails is that you don't spend a lot of time on them. Do them quickly. If you don't like your thumbnail, draw another one. Creating thumbnails is like brainstorming for Web page designers. If you can't complete a thumbnail in 20 to 30 seconds, you're spending too much time on it.

Now it's your turn.

STEP-BY-STEP 5.1

1. Search the Web and pick six Web pages whose looks you like. Choose pages that aren't all the same—ones that have lots of variety on them so they'll be fun to make thumbnails of. List your six choices in Table 5-1 below—listing their titles and their URLs as shown in the sample number 0.

TABLE 5-1
Six visually appealing Web pages

	NAME OF SITE	URL OR WEB ADDRESS
0.	Course Technology	www.course.com
1.		
2.		
3.		
4.		
5.		
6.		

STEP-BY-STEP 5.1 Continued

2. Fold a blank sheet of 8.5 × 11 paper into thirds (like a letter) and then in half.

3. Unfold the paper and number each folded section of paper with the numbers 1 to 6. This will give you a space to do a thumbnail sketch of each of the Web sites you selected above.

4. Quickly do a thumbnail sketch of each of the pages you listed in step 1. This should take less than a minute per sketch. (*Hint:* You don't have to be a great artist to do this.) Save these thumbnail sketches for the next Step-by-Step.

Rough Sketches

Once graphic designers have sketched several ideas as thumbnails, they usually choose one or two of the thumbnails to develop further. Then they draw a better, slightly more developed sketch. They may use a ruler to keep lines straight, make sure the proportions are more accurate, and put a little more detail into the pictures. This more developed sketch is called a *rough sketch*. A rough sketch still uses greeking and very abbreviated lines to represent things, but now they are a little more carefully drawn. Also, the rough sketch is a little larger—from 3 × 5 inches to a full page. Figure 5-3 shows a rough sketch.

FIGURE 5-3
A rough sketch made from a thumbnail sketch

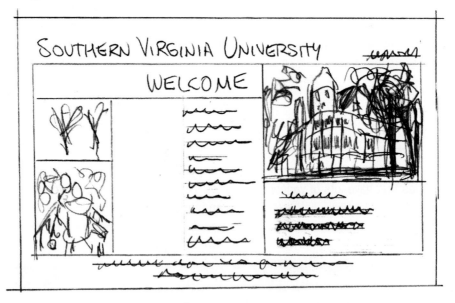

A rough sketch is slightly more developed, but still a sketch. It's a step in the direction of a fully finished design. In the Step-by-Step below, you will take one of your thumbnail sketches and develop it further into a rough sketch.

S TEP-BY-STEP 5.2

1. Select one of the thumbnails you drew in step 4 of the previous Step-by-Step.

2. On a new blank sheet of paper take three to five minutes to create a more carefully drawn version based on one of the thumbnails you drew earlier. *Do not look at the original Web page.* This sketch should be larger and include a few more details and be more cautious about proportions and the relative placement of things on the page. Other than that, it is still a sketch.

3. Once you have finished this rough sketch, compare your sketch to the actual site you were sketching. Since you did this from memory, there are probably some minor differences, but that is not critical. It is important that you see how the rough sketch might guide you in building the Web page at which you are looking.

Choosing a Visual Theme

Up to this point, you've learned the technique for thumbnail and rough sketching by working on images of someone else's Web pages. Now you will use these tools to help you design your own Web site.

You may think that with all the emphasis on content, audience, and structure, you don't have anything left to think about. Actually, everything you've been planning up to this point leads to this final step. You must now select a *visual theme* for your site—or a "look."

Having a visual theme helps you make choices and helps keep the "look and feel" of your site consistent from one page to the next, even though the content from page to page is different. The application of a theme is what brings about style.

Choosing a Theme

Choosing a theme can be the hardest and yet the most fun activity in this book because it can be drawn from virtually anything about which your Web site's content reminds you. Below are a few examples to help get your creative juices flowing. Some of these (like the first two) may be obvious while others (like the latter three) may not be obvious at first but could be a lot of fun.

- If you're doing a Web site about sushi, you may want to make your Web site look like a Japanese restaurant.

- If you're building a Web site about your favorite place to rock climb, a background that looks like rock might be a good "look" for the site.

- If you are doing a Web site on archaeology, you might make your Web site look like an Indiana Jones movie poster, with bright, sweeping orange titles and adventuresome graphics (like a picture of a whip or Indy's hat) because that fictional movie character was an archaeologist.

- In developing a Web site about a 1940s style of clothing, your theme might be the music of the 1940s. Doing so would lead you to choose sights and sounds for your Web site from the music of that era—big bands and jazz.

■   It might be that in doing a Web site about ants, you choose a military theme because ants remind you of soldiers. In this case, you could choose khaki colors and military graphics and stencil fonts that remind you of the Army. You might also put a lot of rigid structure into your site to remind people of the rigid order in the military.

As you can see, your theme can be connected with your content in a variety of ways. The important thing is that the theme should get your audience's attention and communicate your message well. Figure 5-4 illustrates an exceptional themed Web page.

FIGURE 5-4
A themed Web page

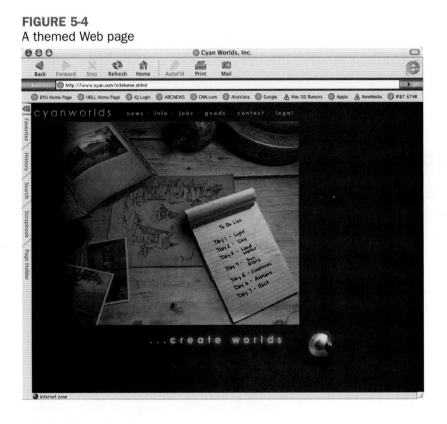

To help you choose a theme for your Web site, start by reviewing your design document. Read all the decisions you have already made (your audience, purpose, message, structure, and so on) and ask, "What does my Web site remind me of? What theme could best contain all of my ideas for this Web site?"

STEP-BY-STEP 5.3

1. Open the design document you created in previous lessons.

2. Create a new heading at the end of your document called **Web Site Theme Ideas**.

3. Take a few minutes with your partner or group to think of every idea you can that is associated with your site. This is a chance for you to brainstorm. While you are brainstorming, there are no bad ideas, so just write everything down. (Do this for every member of the group, if each person is working on different Web site designs.) Often when brainstorming, one idea will lead to another (some people call this "idea hitchhiking"). Use this to generate lots of ideas.

STEP-BY-STEP 5.3 Continued

4. You can stop brainstorming when you have at least six to ten ideas listed in your design document.

5. If it would help make your ideas clearer, you may sketch them as thumbnails. If possible, do both a description and a sketch for each idea. Answer the question "What should this idea look like?".

6. Save your changes to the design document and leave it open for the next Step-by-Step.

Identifying Poor Theme Ideas

When evaluating an idea for a visual theme, use what you think the audience's reaction will be to judge whether it is good or bad. Following are some not-so-great ideas for Web site themes:

■ A site about "new-wave" music might use pictures of the ocean, that is, of "waves," as the theme. This kind of relationship is called a visual pun—new-wave music has nothing to do with the ocean, but we're punning on the word "wave." The problem is that the visual pun is too subtle: The audience will probably not get it. Or if they do, it may make them groan.

■ If someone were trying to make the point that math is fun, they might use a circus theme: bright colors (especially red), clowns, elephants, tents, popcorn. Even though the stated purpose of the site is to show that math is fun, most viewers will miss the connection between "math" and "circus." They'll probably think it makes no sense and be confused by it: "Why is this circus Web site talking about math?"

Once you have lots of good ideas, you must weed out the bad ones from the good ones. Narrow down your ideas and prioritize your top ideas, deleting the rest.

STEP-BY-STEP 5.4

1. Look at the theme ideas you wrote in your design document.

2. Discuss with your group each of these ideas. Point out their good points and bad points and write these down. (Perhaps make a table with "good" and "bad" points or "pros" and "cons.")

3. After you have discussed each theme, select the best six (the ones with no or fewer "bad" points) and delete the rest from your list.

4. Write a number to the left of each of the remaining themes to indicate which ones you like best— 1 for your first choice, 2 for your second choice, and so on.

5. Save your changes to the design document and leave it open for the next Step-by-Step.

Once you have a limited number of ideas to work from (six) you can begin to focus on what they will actually look like. Here's where thumbnail and rough sketches come in handy. In the next Step-by-Step you will make at least one sketch for each one of your ideas. The more thumbnail sketches you can do, the more good ideas from which you will have to choose.

S TEP-BY-STEP 5.5

1. Fold a blank sheet of paper in thirds and then in half, creating six divisions on the page.

2. In the first box, draw a thumbnail sketch of what you think your Web site's welcome page would look like if you applied the first of the six themes you identified in Step-by-Step 5.4.

3. Sketch the second theme's welcome page in the second box, and so on, until you have a welcome page for each theme. As you draw, imagine what your entire Web site might look like based on each of these six themes.

4. Show the six thumbnail sketches to your team and gauge their reactions to your welcome page design ideas.

5. Based on your team's input and your own reaction to your ideas, pick one of the themes to use in the presentation design of your Web site. You may also want to make changes to the theme or the sketch based on your team's comments.

6. Create a new entry in your design document called **Final Theme Decision**.

7. Explain in writing your theme and why you decided to go with that particular theme.

8. Save your design document and leave it open for the next Step-by-Step.

Elements of a User Interface

Now that you have selected a visual theme for your Web site, you must apply the design and create an overall look for your Web site presentation. You will want to plan the pieces or elements that are going to make up the various parts of your page.

Before you begin to apply your visual theme, you must consider three additional elements. Each Web page must have:

- A background that reflects the theme.

- Foreground elements that reflect the theme.

- Other elements that support the theme.

Backgrounds: Colors or Images

On a Web page you have two choices for backgrounds: change the background's color, or add a background graphic. In the case of colors, you simply choose a color, and that is it. However, a background graphic in a Web page is usually *tiled*, that is, repeated over and over again so that it forms a pattern. Because of this, a background graphic is often a texture like rock, paper, or wood. Since either the color or the pattern could overwhelm what is in the foreground, you have to be very careful that you choose colors or pictures that contrast well with whatever you put in front of them. Muted colors or low-contrast images with the colors and highlights (or darks) toned down are best.

In one Web site that the authors were involved with, the subject was fossils. We chose to use an image of a trilobite fossil embedded in rock as the background image, but soon found that the image was "sticking out" and getting in the way of the foreground elements. So we used Photoshop (a photo-editing application software) to reduce the picture's contrast and to lighten it—and it worked great. You can see a resulting Web page in Figure 5-5.

FIGURE 5-5
A trilobite image as a picture and as a background

Foregrounds: Content and Links

The foreground is the page content. It will contain text and images to represent your message to your audience. Some of the text or graphics may be acting as headings, some as content, some as functional parts of the page, such as hyperlinks to other pages. The list of foreground elements might include the elements listed here—some of which are seen in Figure 5-6:

- Titles

- Headings

- Subheadings

- Sidebars

- Body text (the paragraphs that make up the content of the site)

- Illustrations (graphics to support the content of the site)

- Captions (descriptions of the graphics)

FIGURE 5-6
Foreground elements on a Web page

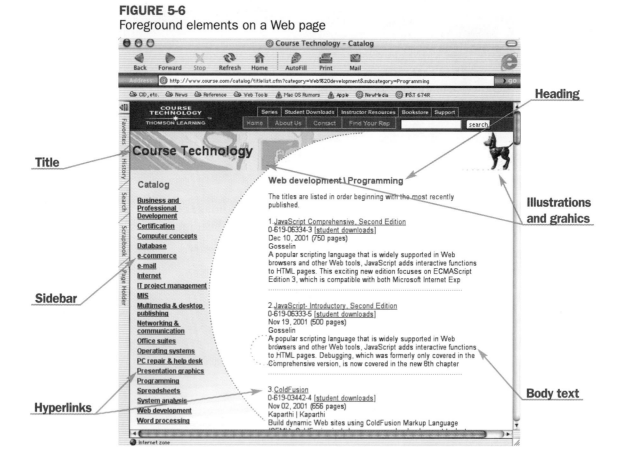

Other Elements

In addition to text and pictures, there may be other elements on a page: buttons, hyperlinks, search fields, navigation bars, a table of contents, and other interactive and navigation elements (see Figure 5-6). These are often created in HTML and JavaScript, useful tools that you may want to learn more about.

Applying Your Theme

The next job in the design process is to apply your selected theme to the elements on your page. When you made your thumbnails and rough sketches, you may have included some of the elements mentioned above. Reading about these elements may have brought other ideas to mind. In this activity, you will redraw your thumbnails for your Web site starting with your welcome page. You will need to construct your theme as you go along. This will give you a chance to brainstorm your visual design in light of the graphic theme you have chosen.

In the previous Step-by-Step you decided on your Web site's theme. In the following Step-by-Step, you will take the time to turn the thumbnail sketches of your Web site pages into rough design drawings. In your rough sketches include any additional elements you may have missed. Use graphics, foreground and background elements, text, and navigation tools that will help you apply the theme to your Web site in a powerful way.

S TEP-BY-STEP 5.6

1. Look at your storyboard pages in your design document.

2. Compare the storyboard pages with the thumbnail sketch you created for the welcome page in the previous Step-by-Step. Think about how your theme can apply across your entire Web site.

3. Count the number of Web pages you have planned in your storyboard. How many pages appear on your storyboard?

4. Fold several sheets of paper into six squares (fold in thirds and then in half) and create as many thumbnail boxes as you have Web pages in your storyboard. (For example, if you have 24 Web pages planned, you will need to fold four sheets of paper.)

5. Create a thumbnail sketch of each Web page you have identified in your storyboard. As you draw, imagine what your individual Web site may look like if you apply your theme to every page. Use your welcome page thumbnail as a guide.

6. In your design document, explain how you have applied your theme to your thumbnail sketches under the heading **Application of the Design Theme to Web Site**. In your description, list and explain the background, foreground, and other elements you have sketched into the thumbnails of your Web site.

7. Save your design document and close it. Save your thumbnail sketches for the next Step-by-Step.

Principles of Design

What makes a "look" work? What's the difference between when something looks good and when it looks bad? Well, there are a few principles you can follow which will make your Web pages look good. If you think about them, they are mostly just common sense. We'll look at three of them: unity, balance, and proportion.

Unity means that all the elements on your page look like they belong together. This is achieved by making them look similar (similar styles or colors) and placing them on the page so that they look "comfortable" around each other.

FIGURE 5-7
Unity: Which of the elements does not seem to belong?

Balance is like a seesaw in a playground. The elements on the page should balance. That doesn't mean that there must be equal weight on both sides (though sometimes it does). On a seesaw, you can have a heavy adult held up by a small child if the child is far out at the end of the seesaw and the adult is near the center on the other side.

Similarly, you can place "light" items (light text, light-colored, or small graphics) far from the center, and have them balance a "heavy" item (large, dark graphics or heavy text) placed closer to the center. Having equally weighted items equally distant from the center results in what is called symmetrical balance; unequally weighted items that are placed so that they balance is called asymmetrical balance—but they're both balanced! Figure 5-8 illustrates these two different types of balance. The centerline (a vertical line down the middle of your screen) can help you balance the elements on your page.

FIGURE 5-8
Balance: Both of these are "balanced." The one on top is symmetrical; the one on the bottom is asymmetrical.

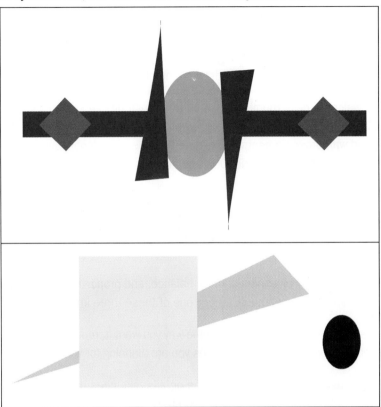

Proportion means things look like they are the right size. You've probably seen drawings by small children in which a person's head is as large as the rest of the whole body. These look funny because they are out of proportion (disproportionate). If you make something large that should be small, or something small that your Web site visitors can tell should be large, the result will be a feeling that something in your site is not quite right (some artists do this on purpose for a humorous effect). Examples might include headings that are too big or too small, graphics that take up too much or too little space on the screen, and so on.

FIGURE 5-9
Proportion: This heading is disproportionately large for the text.

S TEP-BY-STEP 5.7

1. Examine the thumbnails you have created for your Web page. Start with your welcome page thumbnail. Think about how you can convert this thumbnail into a rough design.

2. On a sheet of blank paper, draw rectangles representing the screens to frame your rough sketches. Use a ruler to make them straight, and draw them in black or some other dark color.

3. Transfer your welcome page thumbnail sketch to a rough design sketch. Do this by taking each element and placing it in the appropriate portion of your representative screen. Make sure it lines up and is balanced with other elements. Make sure they are well proportioned to each other and that all of them together form a unified whole. Don't be afraid to redraw this rough sketch several times until you get the page elements "right."

4. Once you have the elements placed and sized appropriately, complete the rough sketch by drawing in the rest of the details of the page. Use colored pencils if you like, or create the rough sketch on a computer with a drawing program.

5. As you draw, try to identify examples of unity, balance, and proportion. On the back of the page, write a short description of where you noticed any one of these three important design principles.

6. Once you have your welcome page designed the way you want it, repeat steps 2 through 5 above to create rough sketches for a few more Web pages you are planning for your Web site.

7. Complete your rough sketches by filling in the details: sketches of graphics or photos, greeking for the text, headings, and so on. Remember you are trying to achieve unity, balance, and proportion. Save your work for the next Step-by-Step.

Having completed your final rough sketches of your Web site, you are ready to build your Web pages. You can use DreamWeaver or another HTML editor or Web authoring tool to help you, or you can create the pages by hand-coding HTML yourself. Whatever tools you decide to use to apply your design, you will have a clear direction, and you will know what you want to see. You can now visualize how your site will look. You may need help creating certain elements of your Web pages, but that's okay. It takes teamwork to create great Web sites.

In the lessons that follow, you will explore how to write the text and how to import graphics into your Web site. Up until now, applying your design may be the most fun you have had. It will be even more exciting to see your Web site theme come together.

Testing Your "Look"

You can follow the rules, you can do everything right, and people still may not like it. That's the problem with the "look" of a thing—everyone has a different opinion. So how do you know if something looks good to your audience? It's simple, really. You ask. You get a bunch of people together, hopefully from your audience, and show them your rough sketches and ask them what they think.

STEP-BY-STEP 5.8

1. Select a collection of your rough sketches to show to your group or another focus group. You should select just a few of the sketches that you feel best represent your entire Web site's "look."

2. Assemble the group and show them the sketches. Fill in the details by describing them to the group. Ask the group to critique the theme as they understand it from looking at the sketches. Make careful notes of the suggestions.

3. Make changes to the sketches and other parts of the design as needed based upon the focus group's recommendations.

4. Create rough sketches for the rest of the Web pages you are planning for your Web site. Complete your rough sketches by filling in the details: sketches of graphics or photos, greeking for the text, headings, and so on. Remember unity, balance, and proportion.

5. Optional: If you have access to a scanner, you may want to scan one or two of your best sketches to add to your design document.

SUMMARY

In this lesson, you learned:

- To use thumbnail sketches and rough sketches to plan your visual design.
- To identify various possible themes for your Web site.
- To plan background, foreground, and other design elements.
- To apply a theme and related design elements to your Web site.
- To apply three principles of design: unity, balance and proportion.
- To use a focus group to test your theme.

VOCABULARY *Review*

Define the following terms:

Balance	Rough sketch	Unity
Greeking	Thumbnail sketch	Visual theme
Proportion	Tiled	

REVIEW *Questions*

TRUE/FALSE

Circle T if the statement is true or F if the statement is false.

T   F   1. Presentation design is sometimes called visual design.

T   F   2. "Greeking" is displaying text in the Greek alphabet.

T   F   3. A bright background with high contrast is best.

T   F   4. In most places, the word "designer" refers to "graphic designers."

T   F   5. "Balance" means things are always exactly the same on both sides.

FILL IN THE BLANK

Complete the following sentences by writing the correct word or words in the blanks provided.

1. A very small sketch, called a(n) _____ sketch, is a designer's way of experimenting with different looks.

2. The very small sketch is often developed into a(n) _____ sketch.

3. The idea for the look of your Web site is called a(n) _____. It helps determine the fonts, colors, etc.

4. Examples of design _____ of a Web site include titles, headings, sidebars, and body text, among other things.

5. One way to test a theme is to use a(n) _____ to see if others think the visual theme looks right.

WRITTEN QUESTIONS

Write a brief answer to the following questions.

1. Why are thumbnail and rough design sketches important to a Web page designer?

2. Why do Web designers use themes to help guide the presentation design of their Web sites?

3. How are balance and proportion related to each other?

4. What is the difference between foreground and background elements? Which should be the most striking and why?

5. In terms of Web design, what does the term "unity" mean?

PROJECTS

PROJECT 5-1

Wally Woodword is about to launch his corporation's Web site at *www.wallywoodworks.com*. However, not being an artist himself, he is concerned about how the Web site will look. He doesn't want to spend a lot of money and end up with an ugly Web site. He has asked you for help. He would like to see some possible thumbnail sketches of how his Web site may appear. Prepare six thumbnail sketches and a rough design sketch of the welcome page for Wally to approve.

TEAMWORK PROJECT

Wally Woodword would like to know what his competition is doing online. Divide into teams of three or four, and use your search skills to find at least five Web pages dedicated to cabinet making, woodworking, or to making furniture for homes. Have each member of the team select one of the sites you have found and sketch its design.

Create a rough design of each of these pages applying what you have learned about Web page elements and the principles of design. Show how space is organized on each Web page. As a team, prepare a presentation for Wally Woodword, demonstrating to him how his site can be made the most attractive and exciting of all the woodworking sites on the Web.

CRITICAL*Thinking*

With what you know about Web design at this point, write a 100-word answer to one or more of the following questions.

SCANS ACTIVITY 5-1

How has your design document helped you keep track of your Web site development plans?

SCANS ACTIVITY 5-2

Now that you have planned the entire scope of your Web site, what resources and talents would you need to create this Web site to your satisfaction? Make a list of the kind of talented people you will need in order to complete an outstanding Web site following your recommendations in your design document.

SCANS ACTIVITY 5-3

Which of these three elements of design do you feel are the most important in the Web site development process: information design, interaction design, or presentation design? Explain your answer.

PLANNING YOUR WEB SITE

REVIEW *Questions*

TRUE/FALSE

Circle T if the statement is true or F if the statement is false.

T F 1. In a linear structure the first page in the line is usually the welcome page.

T F 2. Chunking refers to how broad or narrow your coverage of the topic is.

T F 3. Part of information design is breaking information up into logical pieces called *scope*.

T F 4. Proportion is whether objects are the right size relative to each other.

T F 5. The top page from which all the other pages flow is usually the welcome page in a random access structure.

T F 6. A welcome page is the first page the user typically sees when going to a Web site.

T F 7. One part of navigation is knowing how to get to where you want go.

T F 8. Any page in a hierarchical structure can be a welcome page.

T F 9. One part of navigation is knowing where you are.

T F 10. Unity is when all the elements on the page seem to belong together.

FILL IN THE BLANK

Complete the sentences by writing the correct word or words in the blanks provided.

1. In a(n) _____ sketch you add more detail and proportion to a thumbnail sketch.

2. The _____ structure is the one most commonly used on Web sites.

3. _____ sketches can help you try out lots of different looks for a Web site before actually programming them.

4. When a graphic is _____ that means it is repeated over and over in the background.

5. A good tool for showing the structure of a Web site is by use of a(n) _____.

6. A(n) _____ structure is often used for stories and jokes.

7. A(n) _____ is a tool for organizing structure and relationships in a Web site.

MATCHING

Match the correct term in Column 2 to its description in Column 1.

Column 1	**Column 2**
___ 1. Tries to answer all questions that people building the Web site may have	A. Unity
___ 2. Shows text without writing it all out	B. Chunks
___ 3. Every page available from every other page	C. Purpose
___ 4. When all the elements of a Web page look like they belong together	D. Random access
___ 5. How the user and the Web site work together	E. Scope
___ 6. Who the Web site is written for	F. Message
___ 7. How a user gets around in a Web site	G. Navigation
___ 8. What the site is about	H. Balance
___ 9. Objects on both sides of the screen look to be of equal weight	I. Welcome page
___ 10. Why a Web site exists	J. Audience
	K. Design document
	L. Greeking
	M. Interaction

WRITTEN QUESTIONS

Write brief answers to each of the following questions.

1. What kinds of Web sites would best be put in a random access structure?

2. What kind of Web sites would benefit most from a linear structure?

3. A hierarchical structure would be best for what kind of Web sites?

4. Why are storyboards such a powerful tool in Web page design?

5. What is the purpose of banners and where are they frequently used on Web sites?

6. What purpose do welcome pages serve?

7. What is a context device? Explain these powerful tools with examples.

8. What do thumbnail and rough sketches allow Web page designers to do?

9. How do themes help Web designers in building their Web sites?

10. In terms of Web design what does the term unity mean?

PROJECTS

Throughout Lessons 3, 4, and 5 we have been gradually adding pieces and elements that all belong in the design document. In the following projects you'll be asked to recollect all these pieces and elements.

 PROJECT 1

Go back through Lessons 3, 4, and 5 and identify and list all of the parts of the design document. These may include paragraphs (with their headings), flowcharts, storyboards, sketches, and so forth.

 PROJECT 2

Using the list you created in Project 1, organize the parts of a design document in a logical way according to how each of them fits into a complete design document. Use a word processor to key and print your organized list.

SCANS PROJECT 3

Using the items on the list that you generated in Project 1, write brief descriptions for each of these items. (This outline will be a valuable way for you to remember what you have learned and may give you the information you'll need to create a design document on your own in the future.)

CRITICAL *Thinking*

SCANS ACTIVITY 1

Web site development can take a lot of planning. However, there are classic examples of people who simply sat down at a computer and began building their Web pages off the top of their heads. What are the disadvantages of building a Web site without a design document?

PRODUCING YOUR WEB SITE

Unit 3

Estimated Time for Unit: 11.5 hours

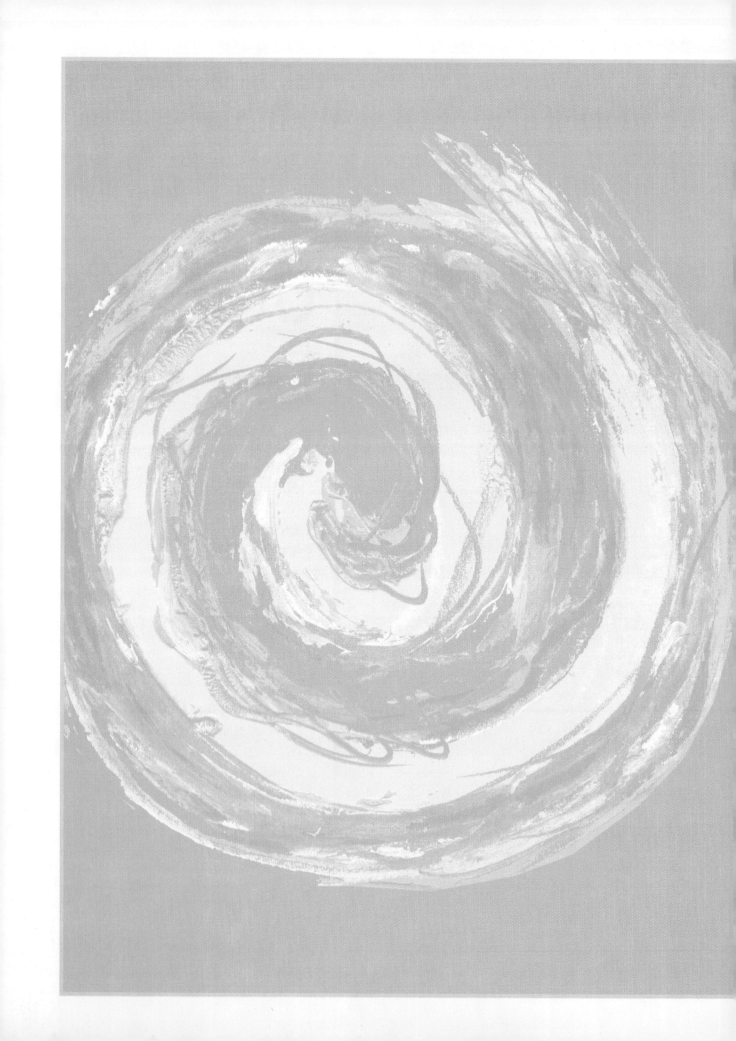

PREPARING YOUR TEXT

OBJECTIVES	VOCABULARY
Upon completion of this lesson, you should be able to: ■ Generate ideas from which to write your text. ■ Create the first draft of your Web site's text. ■ Organize your Web text into an opening, a body, and, if appropriate, a conclusion. ■ Proofread, spell check, and edit your Web pages' text. **Estimated Time: 3 hours**	Body text Concise Conclusion Consistency errors Opening Proofread Rough draft Self-contained text Spell check

Text Flows from the Design

To create a Web site with meaningful information, start with those three parts of information design that we began talking about in Lesson 3: audience, message, and purpose. You have to know what *message* you want to convey to which *audience* in order to fulfill the Web site's *purpose*. In other words, the text of your Web site flows from its basic ideas.

In many ways, the work you did chunking up the information and writing it onto cards is very much what you would do to prepare an outline for a lengthy paper or essay. But because this information will end up in a Web page, there are a couple of differences of which you need to be aware.

One significant difference between writing for the Web and, for example, an English paper is that for the Web, text must be kept to a bare minimum. Nobody likes reading long texts on a computer screen. Your English teacher would call this being **concise**. Think of the last time you encountered a Web page with lots of text. Did you read it all? Unless it was a topic you were *very* interested in, chances are you didn't.

Another difference is that writing for the Web rarely involves producing a single text such as a term paper. Rather, it is writing lots of little texts that are separated onto the various Web pages and are further broken up by pictures and so forth. In other words, the text on a Web page is not only concise, it often has to be **self-contained**, that is, it should not rely on other parts of the text (Web site) to be understood.

STEP-BY-STEP 6.1

1. Take a look at your storyboard, or get out the cards that represent each of the pages on your Web site.

2. If they aren't already numbered, give each card a number, starting with the Welcome card as card number 1.

3. Open a word processor and begin a new document. Call the document (save it as) **Web Text**.

4. Key a number for each of your cards with two returns between each (so that they are double-spaced).

5. After the first number key the following:
- **Purpose:**
- **Message or Idea:**
- **Text:**

6. Select these three lines and copy them. Then paste them after every number so that your document looks like the one in Figure 6-1.

FIGURE 6-1
A Web Text document

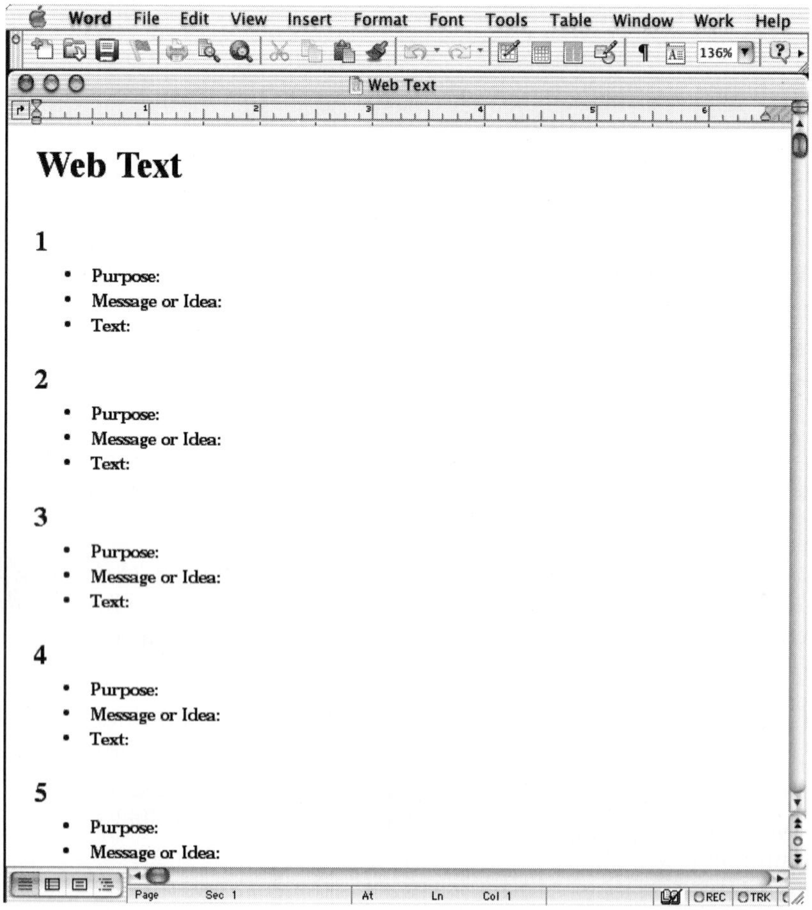

STEP-BY-STEP 6.1 Continued

7. Think about each card in turn. What is the purpose of the Web page that card represents? What message or idea is the Web page meant to convey?

8. For each Web page in your design (each card in your storyboard), key a short description of that Web page's purpose and idea. For example, the welcome page's purpose is to "draw readers further into this Web site"; its message is "Welcome! Look here next."

9. Save your **Web Text** document.

The Importance of Text

Every Web browser in the world is able to display Web page text. Not every Web browser, however, can display Web graphics. In fact, as a service to people with really slow Internet connections, both Netscape Navigator and Microsoft Internet Explorer have a built-in option that lets you view Web pages without having to view (and download) the graphics. If you choose this option, you can later load the images individually. Unless properly handled, graphics are also a problem for visually impaired people. However, they can always "see" the text through special software that reads the text to them. Remember that your Web site's text is the only part of your site that can be viewed by everybody, so it is very important.

Writing a Rough Draft

Remember all those sketches you did before deciding on the final look for your Web page? Well, we are going to do a similar thing for the text. We'll start with a kind of thumbnail of the text, then expand it to the full text, then clean it up and get it ready for your Web site.

A *rough draft* is the thumbnail sketch of text. To start, some writers just put down the first thing that comes to mind on the subject about which they are writing. Others set up imaginary dialogs with people who don't agree with them, and argue their points with these imaginary opponents. Still others organize their thoughts into outlines and spend lots of time perfecting the order before actually turning the ideas in their outlines into full sentences.

At some time or another, most writers have done all these things and many more to get started writing, but in our experience the important thing is to *start*. Once you have something down, it is much easier to *rewrite* than it is to get it right the first time. James Michener, a famous novelist, used to say he was not a very good writer, but that he was a good rewriter.

STEP-BY-STEP 6.2

1. In the previous Step-by-Step you created a document into which you can put all your Web text. If it is not already open, open that file now.

STEP-BY-STEP 6.2 Continued

2. There is a numbered entry in this file for each Web page you are going to build. Look at what you've written for the "Purpose:" and "Message or Idea:" for each entry. Quickly compose a sentence or two that expresses those ideas and write it under the third heading, "Text:" If you find yourself getting carried away and writing more, great! You can edit it down later. Also, if you are building your Web site with a group, you can choose to assign parts of the text to different members of your group.

3. When you have written something for each of the Web pages, go back and ask these questions for each text item:

   a. Is it complete? Does it cover the topic completely?

   b. Will it stand alone? Or, does the reader have to look at other text to understand this one?

   c. Is it clear?

4. Do this for the text for each Web page. These questions will determine the weaknesses in your text. Make changes to your text until you can answer these questions with a "Yes." Often this will mean adding more text to each Web page. (For the moment, go ahead and add more; don't worry about being concise—we'll trim things down later.)

5. When you have written something for each Web page, save your **Web Text** document. It should look something like Figure 6-2.

FIGURE 6-2
A more complete Web Text document

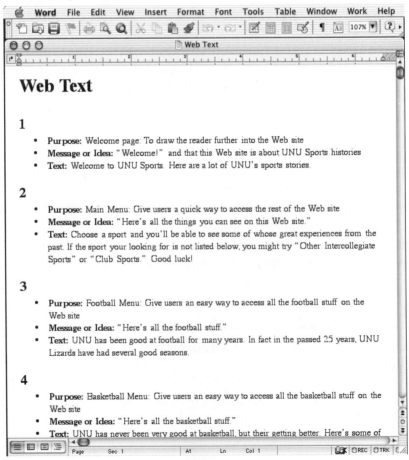

Organizing Your Text

Web pages can be compared to something with which you are already familiar—a term paper. One way in which Web pages and term papers are similar is in their format. Both have an opening, a body, and usually a conclusion. The opening is a sentence or paragraph that introduces your audience to the topic. The body is where you discuss your topic, point by point. Finally, in a conclusion you summarize what you have already said. As you go over the text for each of the pages of your Web site, take time to develop your content according to these guidelines.

The Opening Sentence

The most important part of any Web page—and certainly the most difficult part to write—is the *opening* (sometimes called the introductory sentence). Because the first sentence of your Web page will be one of the first things your audience sees, it is important to get it right.

Another equally important reason that it's important to have a good opening sentence is because the World Wide Web has hundreds of millions of Web pages, and that number is growing daily. In fact, there are so many Web pages available it is almost impossible for anyone to locate a new Web page without the help of a search engine. A search engine is a type of software, usually accessed through a particular Web site (such as www.webcrawler.com), that lets you search the Web for pages whose content contains certain key words or phrases. Those key words and phrases often come from the first sentence.

Table 6-1 gives examples of both good and bad first sentences. Look at each carefully and try to figure out what is wrong with the "bad" sentences and why the "good" sentences are effective.

> **Thinking about Technology**
>
> Thanks to the World Wide Web, you now have the ability to access tens of millions of documents around the world. You may be tempted to "borrow" text or ideas from some of these documents as you develop your Web site. If you do borrow text or an idea from another document, you must document it just as if you had copied it from a book. In other words, you must give credit where credit is due. Plagiarism is the stealing of texts or ideas from someone without giving credit. Plagiarism is stealing, whether the material is printed or presented online. Why do you think it is unethical to borrow text or an idea from another document without giving credit? What harm could result from your doing this?

TABLE 6-1
Examples of bad and good opening sentences

BAD FIRST SENTENCES	GOOD FIRST SENTENCES
This is my first Web page; I've never done one before.	This Web page tells you everything you could ever want to know about the 1979 Pittsburgh Steelers.
I like mittens.	Welcome to the mitten home page, your one-stop shop for all your mitten needs.
This is the introduction to my Web page about Web page writing.	This page demonstrates the elements of good Web page text authoring: a good introductory sentence, well thought-out body text, and a short summary of the topics presented.
To find out more about us, read this.	Read on to learn more about Union High School's Renegade Regiment marching band.
I hope to get a good grade in school.	This Web page explains the time-honored secrets to earning good grades.

You have already written something for each Web page that may stand as the opening sentence. If there were nothing else but the introductory sentence on your page, would your intended audience know they were in the right place? If so, you're getting closer to a good introductory sentence.

The Body Text

Once you have a good introductory sentence, the next part of the text is the main text of each Web page. Like the *body text* of a term paper or report, the body text of each Web page contains the detailed facts, comments, and information you want to share with your audience.

As you write each Web page's main text, keep your audience in mind and make sure that everything you write focuses on meeting their needs. You need to remember that most of your audience may not know as much about your topic as you do. So, if there is a chance that someone in your audience will not understand part of your Web text, either explain that part in full or don't write it. You should write your body text so that it is understandable to even the most novice readers.

For example, pretend that you are writing a Web page that focuses on NASA. A good Web text would explain that NASA stands for the National Aeronautics and Space Administration (and a *really* good Web text would explain a little of NASA's history—possibly as a link to a separate page).

One last thing to remember as you write your body text is that the Web is international. Writing something like "hop on the interstate and beeline-it to the nearest 7 Eleven" will probably make no sense to someone outside the United States. (After all, there are no Interstates or 7 Elevens in Germany, and besides, why would you "hop" on a highway? And how do you "beeline-it"?) If your audience is international, make sure that your Web page's body text includes language that others will understand.

The Conclusion

The last part of a Web text is a *conclusion*, where you bring together the points you made earlier. With Web pages, the conclusion is optional (many Web page designers omit it altogether). The decision on whether or not to include a conclusion should be based on what you think your audience will need.

Rules for Web Page Writing

Following are some rules of good Web page writing:

- Know your audience.
- Your message needs to match your audience.
- If there is a chance that someone in your audience will not understand a certain part of your Web page, either explain that part in full or don't write it.
- A good Web text will have an opening, a body, and probably a conclusion.
- Keep things as concise as possible.
- Keep text self-contained, if possible.

Net Tip

Should you key your Web page's text in a word processor such as Microsoft Word or Corel WordPerfect, or in a Web page editor program such as Macromedia Dreamweaver or Adobe GoLive? The answer is: Use a word processor—they are designed for handling the manipulation of words and have the features to more easily do so (for example, powerful spell checkers and grammar checkers). After you have written and refined the text, you can import or copy and paste it into the HTML editor.

Thinking about Technology

What would happen if you did not identify the audience for the Web sites you create? Would not identifying your audience make choosing a message easier or harder? Give an example of a Web site whose message is so universal that its creators need not worry about identifying its audience. Is this example the exception or the rule?

STEP-BY-STEP 6.3

1. If your **Web Text** document is not already open, open it now.

2. Look at the text for one of the pages you have written so far. Check to see if there is an opening sentence.

3. If there is not an opening for the page you are looking at either rearrange the sentences so that one of them can be the opening, or write an opening. Use Table 6-1 for examples of good openings.

4. Look at the body of that same text. Ask yourself the following questions:
   a. Is it complete?
   b. Does it meet the needs of my audience?

5. If you answered "no" to either of the questions in step 4, rewrite your body text.

6. If your Web text has a conclusion, ask yourself,
   a. Does it draw my ideas together well?
   b. Would this Web text be better without it?

7. Write, rewrite, or eliminate your conclusion depending on your answers to the questions in step 6.

8. Repeat steps 2 through 7 for every Web text in your file.

9. Save your **Web Text** document file.

When you have finished Step-by-Step 6.3, you will have a document that looks something like Figure 6-3.

FIGURE 6-3
Web Text document containing first drafts

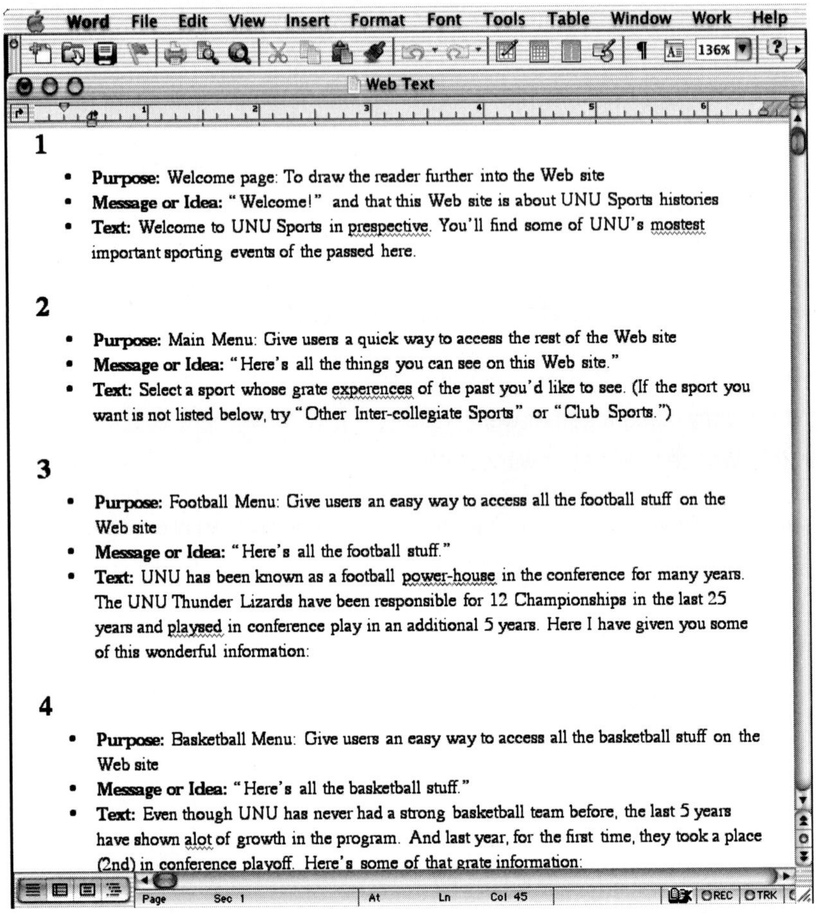

Word File Edit View Insert Format Font Tools Table Window Work Help

Web Text

1

- **Purpose:** Welcome page: To draw the reader further into the Web site
- **Message or Idea:** "Welcome!" and that this Web site is about UNU Sports histories
- **Text:** Welcome to UNU Sports in prespective. You'll find some of UNU's mostest important sporting events of the passed here.

2

- **Purpose:** Main Menu: Give users a quick way to access the rest of the Web site
- **Message or Idea:** "Here's all the things you can see on this Web site."
- **Text:** Select a sport whose grate experences of the past you'd like to see. (If the sport you want is not listed below, try "Other Inter-collegiate Sports" or "Club Sports.")

3

- **Purpose:** Football Menu: Give users an easy way to access all the football stuff on the Web site
- **Message or Idea:** "Here's all the football stuff."
- **Text:** UNU has been known as a football power-house in the conference for many years. The UNU Thunder Lizards have been responsible for 12 Championships in the last 25 years and playsed in conference play in an additional 5 years. Here I have given you some of this wonderful information:

4

- **Purpose:** Basketball Menu: Give users an easy way to access all the basketball stuff on the Web site
- **Message or Idea:** "Here's all the basketball stuff."
- **Text:** Even though UNU has never had a strong basketball team before, the last 5 years have shown alot of growth in the program. And last year, for the first time, they took a place (2nd) in conference playoff. Here's some of that grate information:

Editing Your Text

Congratulations. You have written a complete first draft of your Web site's text. Now it is time for you to "clean it up." This is actually a simple process, but it is one that many inexperienced Web page designers overlook.

Step One: Spell Check and Proofread

One of the quickest ways to annoy your audience (and often lose their interest) is to write Web pages that use poor grammar or contain misspelled words. After all, would you trust a Web page that told you that "the bestest way to make mony fast iz too purchase our mony-making producks"?

Thinking about Technology

Think about some of the papers or reports you have recently written. Would any of them make good Web pages? What changes would you have to make to these papers or reports to ensure they appeal to the general public that surfs the Web? What changes would you have to make to be sure that your papers or reports are understandable to international readers? What problems could arise from just putting your old papers and reports on the Web without rewriting them for the Web?

So, the first and most crucial step in the editing process is to *spell check* your Web page's text. Fortunately, most word processors (such as Corel WordPerfect and Microsoft Word) and even some HTML editor programs (such as Adobe GoLive and Macromedia Dreamweaver) offer built-in spell checkers.

But beware! Spell checkers do not know the difference between one word and another, so they will not catch a correctly spelled wrong word. For example there are seven spelling errors in the following sentence, but every word is spelled correctly!

I all ready tolled you to times that you're too friends aren't already for there class.

It is a good idea to carefully examine each sentence in your Web page for misspelled and mis-used words. Following are some commonly misspelled or misused words:

- *You* and *Your.* This is a frequent typographical error on Web pages (as well as in other text), and spell checkers will not catch it. A good example of this error appears in the sentence, "You need to make sure that you message matches your audience."

- *Two, To,* and *Too. Two* is a number; *to* is a preposition; and *too* means "also."

- *There, They're,* and *Their. There* is a direction or place; *they're* is a contraction of "they are"; and *their* means "belonging to them."

- *Its* and *It's. Its* means "belonging to it"; *it's* is a contraction for "it is."

- *You're* and *Your. You're* is short for "you are" or "you were"; *your* means "belonging to you."

- *All ready* and *Already. All ready* means to be completely prepared; *already* means "previously."

And that sentence we looked at above? Here it is with the errors corrected:

I already told you two times that your two friends aren't all ready for their class.

Spell checkers will also miss **consistency errors**. A consistency error occurs when you change your writing style from paragraph to paragraph or from sentence to sentence. The two biggest consistency errors involve pronoun use and contraction use.

- *Pronoun Use.* Starting a page in a plural voice ("we are glad you chose to visit our Web page") and then switching to singular ("if you have any questions, contact me at..."). Pick singular (I, me, mine, and so on) or plural (we, us, our, and so on), and then stick with that voice throughout your Web pages.

- *Contraction Use.* Switching between using contractions (I've, won't, you're) and not using contractions (I have, will not, you are). If you use contractions, use them throughout your Web site; if you don't use contractions, avoid them consistently.

Run a careful spell check on your Web text and do a careful read-through to check for misused words, grammar problems, typographical errors, and consistency errors.

Step Two: Clean It Up and Weed It Out

The second step in the editing process is to make sure everything is clear, and then remove as many words as you can from your Web page. This may seem

Did You Know?

To ensure a consistent style in every keyed document they produce, most major newspapers use style guides. A style guide is a rule book that shows reporters how certain words are to be spelled, to be capitalized, or even to be used in their stories. Two of the most popular style guides are the *Associated Press Stylebook and Libel Manual* and the *Chicago Manual of Style,* which you can purchase in most major bookstores.

strange, especially after you just expanded your narrative in Step-by-Step 6.3. The reason you need to edit your text, though, is to save your audience's time. After all, why say "After careful consideration of the entire situation, I have decided to decline your offer" when you can just as easily say "Sorry, no"?

E. B. White said it in just four words: "Make every word tell." White was a highly educated professional writer. But notice how concise his sentence is, and how simple his words are. One way to make things better: Take out every big word and replace it with a shorter, simpler word. Better yet, just take them all out. Often, they won't be missed.

Following is a good example of how you can save your audience's time through editing.

Original Paragraph (150 words):

Writing a Web page is pretty easy. The only trick is that you have to know a few simple rules. One of the most important rules is that you have to know your audience. Once you have identified your audience, you need to make sure that the message of your Web page matches your audience. After you have done that, you need to realize that if it would be easier on the audience if you divided your information into two or more pages, then divide your information into two or more pages. Of course, the opposite of this is true as well: if you don't need to divide your information into different Web pages, then you don't have to. Finally, if there is a chance that someone in your audience will not understand a certain part of your Web page, either explain that part in full or don't write it.

New Paragraph (58 words):

Writing a Web page is easy, provided you follow a few rules. First, know your audience and match your message to your audience. Second, if you can easily divide your Web page's information into two or more pages, do it. Finally, make sure that the information on your Web page is understandable to everyone who may view it.

Both paragraphs say the same thing, but the second one is shorter and much easier to read.

Look at your Web page text and carefully rework phrases and words until you have edited it down to a readable, essential core.

Step Three: Spell Check and Proofread Again

Now that you have radically changed your Web page's text, it is a good idea to spell check it and *proofread* it again. In fact, it is at this step that many professional Web designers spell check their text, proofread it, and then ask someone else to proofread their text. (Having someone else read it will catch errors that you cannot see because you've read the text so many times.)

> ### Did You Know?
>
> *The New York Times* is so adamant about maintaining a consistent writing style throughout its newspaper that its editors scour every article its reporters have written, looking for anything that violates the writing rules established in the newspaper's style guide.

S TEP-BY-STEP 6.4

1. If necessary, open your **Web Text** document.

2. Perform a spell check of the text and make any necessary corrections.

3. Proofread your text looking for any misused words or consistency errors and make whatever edits are necessary.

STEP-BY-STEP 6.4 Continued

4. Reread your Web text and look for any ways in which you can make it cleaner and more concise. Rewrite any sentences or paragraphs as you see fit.

5. Perform a spell check on your text again and make any additional corrections.

6. Proofread your text again, paying special attention to the text that you edited.

7. Ask a classmate to proofread your text for you and to make suggestions for improvements.

8. Make any additional changes that would improve your Web text based upon the feedback from your classmate.

9. Save your document, print it, and close your word processor.

Once you have completed Step-by-Step 6.4, your document may look something like the Web text document that is shown in Figure 6-4. It should be free of any spelling or grammatical errors, it should clearly convey your ideas, and it should be as concise as possible while still adequately providing the information.

FIGURE 6-4
A completed Web Text document

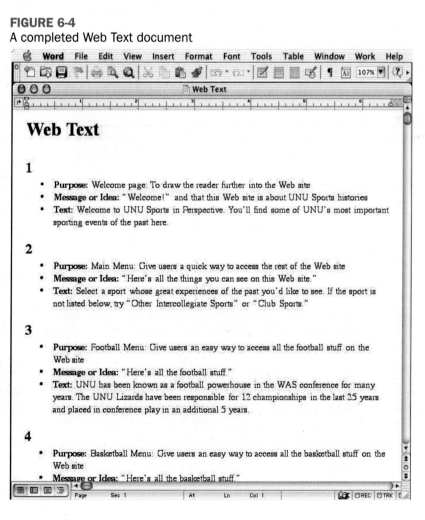

Using the Web to Help with Grammar and Spelling

Many people are not good at spelling or grammar. If you are one of these people, you may not be sure about what is correct and incorrect in the text of your Web page. Fortunately, the Web can help you answer any questions you may have concerning proper use of the language. Suppose you have a question concerning grammar. The Step-by-Step 6.5 illustrates how you could use the Web to find an answer to your question.

S TEP-BY-STEP 6.5

1. Connect to the Internet if necessary and open your Web browser.

2. Key the following address in the appropriate address box: **www.yahoo.com**.

3. Key in the search text **English Grammar Usage** and click on the **Search** button.

4. When the search is complete, click on the **English Language> Grammar, Usage, and Style** category.

5. Click on a link that focuses on a specific question you may have.

6. Once you have found the answer to your question(s), close the browser and disconnect from the Internet if necessary.

If your question is about spelling or the definition of a word, you might visit the following address instead: *www.m-w.com/dictionary.htm*. This is the Merriam-Webster online dictionary. Or you could search for the keywords "English dictionary."

Net Tip

Remember that a Web address may change at any time. An address given in this book as an example may no longer be valid. If this is so, do a search to find the site or one that is similar.

A Sample Text Editing Activity

To understand how audience, message, and organization all come together to affect content, let's take a look at an example. The Bertrand Russell Intermediate High School Concert Choir has decided to create its own Web site.

The following is the first draft of the Web page that focuses on meeting the needs of the people interested in attending future choir performances. Use what you have learned to find problems in this text. Check for a strong opening sentence, spelling, grammar, consistency, and complete information.

Concert Choir. The Concert Choir will be performing again soon. Our next performance will be on August 7th. The performance will start at 7:00 PM. The performance will be held in the high school auditorium. The performance will be a caucophony of melodic and symphonic gloriosity. We'd love to see you there. If you have any questions, call me. Click here for prices.

OK, let's go through this text keeping in mind what we have learned in this lesson.

- Obviously, that first sentence has to go. The opener "Concert Choir" does not tell you specifically which Concert Choir, or tell you what the page's topic is, nor does it particularly inspire interest in what this particular Web page has to offer. A much better first sentence would be something like: "The Bertrand Russell Intermediate High School Concert Choir proudly presents its latest concert extravaganza."

- The next four sentences (the body of the text) have a few problems as well. While these sentences contain a lot of words, they don't offer much solid information. What day of the week is August 7th? How do you get to the high school auditorium?

- The fifth sentence—"The performance will be a caucophony of melodic and symphonic gloriosity"—is downright silly. It contains one misspelled and misused word (cacophony means "noise") and one made-up word.

- The last two sentences suffer from consistency errors. One sentence uses the word "we" and the next uses the word "me."

- If you want readers to call, why haven't you given them a phone number? In the sentence about prices, why are prices on another page? The prices and contact information should be included here to make the text complete and self-contained.

- Wouldn't "We'd love to see you there!" make a great conclusion? It definitely sums up the purpose of the text. It would be better if it were moved to the end.

Cleaned up, the text for this Web page would read much better as:

The Bertrand Russell Intermediate High School Concert Choir proudly presents its latest concert extravaganza. Our next performance will be on Thursday, August 7th, in the high school auditorium (6636 South Mingo Road). Prices are $3 for adults, $2 for students. If you have any questions, please call us at 555-1212. We'd love to see you there!

That's it. It's much better now.

SUMMARY

In this lesson, you learned:

- To generate ideas from which to write your text.
- To create the first draft of your Web site's text.
- To organize your Web text into an opening, a body, and, when appropriate, a conclusion.
- To proofread, spell check, and edit your Web pages' text.

VOCABULARY *Review*

Define the following terms:		
Body text	Consistency errors	Rough draft
Concise	Opening	Self-contained text
Conclusion	Proofread	Spell check

REVIEW *Questions*

TRUE/FALSE

Circle T if the statement is true or F if the statement is false.

T　F　1. There is no connection between knowing your audience and writing good text for a Web site.

T　F　2. The longer the sentence, the better it will be because it will be complete.

T　F　3. A rough draft is to writing what a thumbnail sketch is to a drawing or picture.

T　F　4. Your opening sentence should help draw the reader into the rest of your text.

T　F　5. The body text is where the details are located.

FILL IN THE BLANK

Complete the following sentences by writing the correct word or words in the blanks provided.

1. Writing for the Web should always be as _____ as possible.

2. Web text should be _____, meaning that it does not need to refer to any other text to be understood.

3. The first version of the text you put down is called a(n) _____.

4. Three parts to a Web text are the _____, _____, and an optional _____.

WRITTEN QUESTIONS

Write a brief answer to each of the following questions.

1. What is the benefit of writing a rough draft and then correcting it rather than just writing it correctly in the first place?

2. Why is your Web page's introductory sentence so important? (Give at least two reasons.)

3. Improve the following sentence: "In the very short time span of about four or five years, the World Wide Web (usually called the Web) went from a way for scholars and scientists to share scientific papers to a new kind of mass communications medium like television or magazines or newspapers or radio." (*Hint:* Think about E. B. White's phrase, "Make every word tell.")

4. Why are short words better than long ones?

5. How could knowing your Web site's audience help determine what your Web site's message is going to be? Give an example.

PROJECTS

PROJECT 6-1

With your instructor's help, identify three Web sites that are content-oriented, that is, they are not just indexes or lists of links but contain content. On each site, find at least one page containing content text and analyze it. Answer the following questions:

1. Does the text have an opening, a body, and, if appropriate, a conclusion?

2. Is the text clear and concise? Is the text self-contained; can it stand alone without further explanation?

3. Is the text grammatically correct? Does it contain misspelled words or consistency errors?

Repeat this process for each of the three Web sites.

PROJECT 6-2

Rewrite the texts you found in Project 6-1 so that they answer the questions correctly. If they are already well written, identify how specific parts of the text meet the criteria mentioned above.

TEAMWORK PROJECT

For this project, select one of the Web sites from Project 6-1. Imagine that your group or team has been hired as a group of consultants to review this Web site. Your present focus will be on the text in the Web site. View the Web site as a group and identify at least three texts in the Web site for discussion.

As a group, try to identify who you think the target audience is for the Web page. Then discuss whether the text appropriately meets the needs of its target audience. If it doesn't, discuss how it could be improved. Remember, you're only analyzing the text—not the entire site. Prepare a written report of your findings to submit to the "client."

CRITICAL*Thinking*

ACTIVITY 6-1

With what you know about Web design at this point, write a 100-word response to the following: If a picture is said to be worth a thousand words, give five reasons why you think the text content of a Web site is more important than its graphics.

THE WHYS AND WHEREFORES OF WEB GRAPHICS

Graphics Made the Web Popular

Can you imagine the Web without graphics? Most people can't, but the original Web browsers allowed only text. It wasn't until 1994, starting with a software program called Mosaic, that browsers began to allow *inline graphics*; that is, graphics in the same window as the text. The Mosaic project was housed at the University of Illinois at Urbana-Champaign. One computer science student who worked on Mosaic was Marc Andreessen.

Andreessen went on to help create one of the most influential Internet-based companies, Netscape Communications Corporation, which is now part of America Online. Netscape later replaced Mosaic with a more powerful and efficient graphical browser called Netscape Navigator. In the years that followed the release of Mosaic and Netscape Navigator, Microsoft created its Internet Explorer (IE) browser, which also allowed inline graphics. Today both of these browsers display graphics brilliantly and can present other multimedia elements in exciting ways.

To make your Web pages communicate well, you will also want to add graphics to them. It is important to make sure that your graphics look good and that they enhance, not get in the way of, your message.

The Roles Graphics Play

Graphics can have several different roles in a Web page, but the most common are for them to be:

- Part of the message
- Part of the user interface and navigation
- Part of the theme

Because graphics affect the speed of download, you should always have a good reason for using a graphic image. Each graphic must have a purpose. In fact, some graphics can have more than one purpose. For example, it is not uncommon for a graphic image to be part of the user interface while at the same time enhancing the theme of the Web page.

Graphics as Part of the Message

Graphics that are part of the message tend to be:

- Large
- Photographic or detailed
- Important

When graphics are the message itself, they tend to take up a large share of the screen. In other words, when the message the Web page is intended to communicate is best said with a picture, it is OK to use a large graphic. In fact, some Web pages have nothing but pictures with just a small amount of descriptive text, such as the painting in Figure 7-1.

FIGURE 7-1
This Web page includes an image that is part of the message

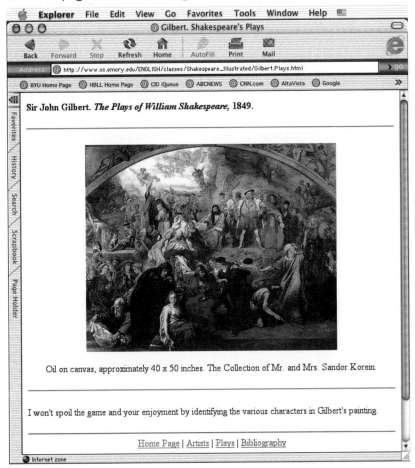

Sir John Gilbert. *The Plays of William Shakespeare*, 1849.

Oil on canvas, approximately 40 x 50 inches. The Collection of Mr. and Mrs. Sandor Korein.

I won't spoil the game and your enjoyment by identifying the various characters in Gilbert's painting.

Home Page | Artists | Plays | Bibliography

Imagine that you just dropped in from another planet and someone here was trying to help you understand what a cat is. What would be more informative: a photograph of a cat or a description of a cat? For the space on the page, a photograph would probably tell you much more than a written description. Some things are best understood with photographs.

Photographic images tend to be detailed. Often when Web graphics are the message, they are photograph-like, providing lots of detail like a photograph. The camera does not leave things out selectively; the added detail lends reality and additional value to the graphic.

We've all heard the saying, "A picture is worth a thousand words." We'd like to modify that somewhat—the *right* picture is worth *at least* a thousand words. (The wrong picture may take a thousand words to explain, but it isn't worth very much.) That is why a good picture (one that is relevant to your subject) is definitely worth a lot.

It is a sad fact that many people will not plow through too much text on a computer screen unless they're *really* interested in it. But because our minds react to visual stimuli, you can provide a lot of information and evoke a lot of emotion with a picture. The images you choose can supply the most important part of your message.

Representations

A graphic that depicts something real is called a *representation*. If you created a Web site about the performance of a play, you might use pictures of the cast members in their costumes to show who was in the play. In this instance, the pictures are representations of the people in the play, since you can't have the live actors themselves hanging around for the advertising.

Generally, when a graphic is standing in for something, it is a representation. Sometimes a picture represents a group of things or a type of thing. For example, if a Web site contained pictures of animals, you can probably guess what clicking on individual graphics of a dog, cat, and fish would lead to.

The neat thing about representations is that they are usually pretty easy to understand. They can often stand alone without any other explanation. Graphics as representations are most often used as part of the message of the Web page.

Graphics as User Interface and Navigation Elements

It is always attractive to have nice graphics serve as your user interface and navigation elements.

User interface elements let you know where you are in the Web site and where you can go (see Lesson 4). User interface elements are often *icons*; small symbolic graphics that help the Web page visitor understand what each will do when selected. For instance, on your browser toolbar, you probably have a Print icon—it looks like a printer. To make obscure icons a little more clear, icons are often accompanied by text, such as the word *Print* under the icon. To find graphic images that are user interface elements, ask yourself, "Which graphics help me know where I am or where I can go?" Figure 7-2 is an example of graphics being used as user interface elements.

FIGURE 7-2
Graphics that look like folder tabs often serve as user interface elements

Home | Forums & Chat | Site of the Day | Shopping | Games

Another kind of graphics often overlooked by beginners is *text graphics*. These are often banners. Because the fonts and kinds of text that can be displayed on a Web page are limited, text is often converted to a graphic image. This technique allows the designers to create very attractive text and logos with some special effects. Of course, the downside to using text graphics is that they download much more slowly than plain text. But it is a price most Web designers are willing to pay to achieve the look they want for a Web page.

Symbols

Symbols are more abstract than representations. A symbol is a graphic that represents something but doesn't necessarily act like or look like the thing it represents. Sometimes the thing being represented is something abstract, such as an idea. For example, a stop sign doesn't look like "stop", it symbolizes it.

Imagine you are making a Web site devoted to Shakespeare's plays. One way to organize the content is to divide the plays into three major types: comedies, tragedies, and histories. You might use the classic happy and sad Greek masks to indicate the tragedies and comedies. An icon of a book might be appropriate for the histories. These icons can be seen in Figure 7-3.

FIGURE 7-3
Greek comedy and tragedy masks and a book can be used as icons

Because symbols are more abstract, there is the possibility that they will be misunderstood. For that reason, if the symbols are being used as buttons, you may want to include words to clarify the symbols. Symbols are most often used as user interface elements (like buttons).

Graphics as Part of the Theme

Graphics that enhance a Web site's theme are a little more difficult to spot than graphical banners and navigation icons. For many Web sites, the "look" is more important than anything else (such as Web sites that are trying to sell something stylish). In these cases, designers often include big, beautiful graphics that serve no other purpose than to enhance the theme or "style" of the page. Figure 7-4 is an illustration of such a Web site. The graphics on this page are here solely to match the pyramid theme. Note that the font used on the page also matches the theme.

FIGURE 7-4
Graphics as part of the theme

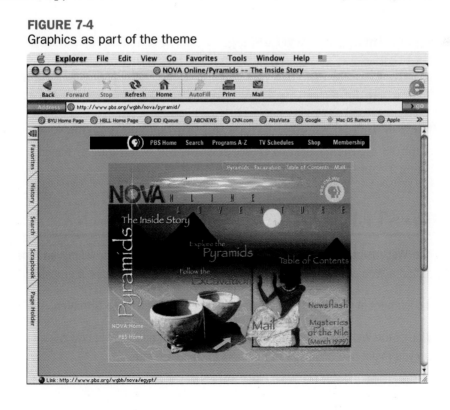

When you are looking for graphics that are part of the Web page's content, you must ask, "Which graphics add to the *message* of the page?" To discover graphics that are thematic or stylistic, ask, "Which of these adds to the 'look' or theme of the Web page?"

Metaphors

A simile or *metaphor* is saying that something is like something else. If you say a computer is like a brain, you're using a metaphor; what you mean is that the computer works like a brain.

A good example of a metaphor is the trash can icon or recycling icon on your computer, such as the one shown in Figure 7-5. When you drag a file to that icon, it deletes the file. The use of a trash can icon builds on things you know (what a trash can looks like, what happens to things that get put into it) to help you understand things you may not (that by deleting a file, you are actually reassigning the memory space allocated to that file in a memory table to represent free memory available for future storage use).

FIGURE 7-5
The trash can on a Macintosh

A good metaphor can apply to several things at once. For example, Windows or Macintosh operating systems use a variety of metaphors combined into one large metaphor of an office (not only a recycling bin but a desktop where you work, folders to put things in, and an hourglass or wristwatch to tell you to be patient and wait). Unfortunately, even the best metaphor breaks down. For instance, on a computer you use windows to hold documents that you are working on; in a real office you use real windows to look out of when you're trying to avoid work!

Graphic metaphors are the hardest to create and use, but when they are used, they often communicate something about the theme.

STEP-BY-STEP 7.1

1. Search the Web using your favorite Internet search engine or by browsing an index site such as Yahoo! to find a Web page you like that uses a large image to dominate its message.

2. Create a document in your word processor and save it as **Web Page Graphics**.

3. List the title of the Web page and its URL in your document and explain how the image is used. Think about how you might use an image of this sort in your Web site.

STEP-BY-STEP 7.1 Continued

4. Find a Web page you like that uses a photographic image.

5. List the title of the Web page and its URL in your document and explain how the image is used. Think about how you might use an image of this sort in your Web site.

6. Find a Web page you like that uses graphics to visually demonstrate that some specific element has great importance.

7. List the title of the Web page and its URL in your document, and explain how the images are used. Think about how you might use images this way in your Web site.

8. Search the Web for a page you like that uses graphics to expertly facilitate navigation and user interactions.

9. List the title of the Web page and its URL in your document and explain how the graphics are used. Think about how you might use these sorts of images in your Web site.

10. Find a Web page you like that uses a graphic to display text, as in its banner.

11. List the title of the Web page and its URL in your document and explain how the graphic text is used. Think about how you might use graphic text in your Web site.

12. Find a Web page you like that uses graphics that are directly related to the Web site's theme.

13. List the title of the Web page and its URL in your document and briefly describe how theme-related graphics work.

14. Save your document and close it.

15. Review your storyboard and rough sketches created in earlier lessons. Have you learned anything in this activity that can help you improve your use of graphics on these pages? Are there any changes you would like to make? If so, open your design document and describe these changes under a new heading called **Improving the Graphics**.

16. If necessary, save your changes to your design document; then close it and your word processor.

Computer Graphic Fundamentals

Creating artwork on a computer is very different from using other media such as watercolors or oil painting. Computer graphics use very different color schemes, and the images show only a limited amount of detail. On the other hand, Web graphics are usually bright, and if you like, the pictures can be animated to show movement. These differences are sometimes a challenge for an artist, but once you learn to use computer graphics tools, Web graphics can be a lot of fun to create.

Thinking about Technology

Web pages are not the only media created by computers that use graphics. Magazines (and many books) are developed on computers. Look at the pages of a popular magazine. In articles, do the images tend to be part of the message, serve as user interface elements, or add to the theme? How about the use of graphics in advertisements? Do graphics on advertising pages tend to be part of the message, serve as user interface elements, or add to the theme?

Pixels

When you paint, you spread colored material on paper or canvas. You don't often worry that the paint will form lumps that people can see, but that's exactly what happens on a computer because computer pictures are made up of tiny, almost visible dots. If the dots were any bigger, you could see them easily. These dots are called *pixels*. The word pixel is short for "*picture element.*" Viewed with a magnifying glass on your monitor, pixels look like little mosaics. Figure 7-6, a magnified view of the Internet Explorer icon, allows you to see the pixels that make up this icon. Compared to paint, or even this book, a computer screen has a very low level of *resolution* (that is, the number of pixels or dots in a given space is a very small number compared to the number of dots in the same space in a printed document).

FIGURE 7-6
The Internet Explorer icon magnified to show pixels

Resolution is measured in dots per inch (dpi) or sometimes in pixels per inch (ppi). When creating graphics for computer monitors (as in Web pages), you should save all your pictures at a resolution of 72 dpi. (In Windows, you can use 96 dpi if you wish—they are functionally identical.) This resolution is what most computer monitors display. Therefore, making a Web graphic 300 dpi might make it look good on paper, but it's wasted on a Web page because the monitor displays it at 72 dpi anyway and ignores all that other information.

In the following Step-by-Step, we use Adobe Photoshop to make some changes to a high-resolution image. Photoshop is one of the most popular graphics programs for computers, and it is available for both Windows and Macintosh computers. If you do not have Photoshop available, some of the steps may not be available in your graphics program, or they may appear differently. Ask your instructor for assistance in completing the steps with the software you have available, or use the Help available to find out how to complete the tasks. As you learn to use your own graphic software, you will become more aware of its power and its limitations.

S TEP-BY-STEP 7.2

1. Open Adobe Photoshop if it is available, or open another photo-editing application. (Ask your instructor if you are unsure of what program you should use.)

2. Open **Step7-2.tif**. This is a high-resolution picture.

3. Save this image as **Web Picture.jpg**.

4. Click **Image** on the menu bar and then click **Image Size** to open the Image Size dialog box. (Don't confuse this with the Canvas Size command!)

STEP-BY-STEP 7.2 Continued

5. If they are not already set, change the **Document Size** measurements to inches by using the drop-down menus.

6. Change **Document Size** numbers to sizes that would be appropriate for a picture accompanying text on a Web page—say 3 inches wide. If you have constrain proportions set, you'll notice that when you change one print size number, the other changes to keep the picture proportional.

7. Set the resolution to **72 dpi**—an appropriate resolution for a Web page. When finished your changes should look something like Figure 7-7.

FIGURE 7-7
Image Size dialog box with the print size and resolution changes

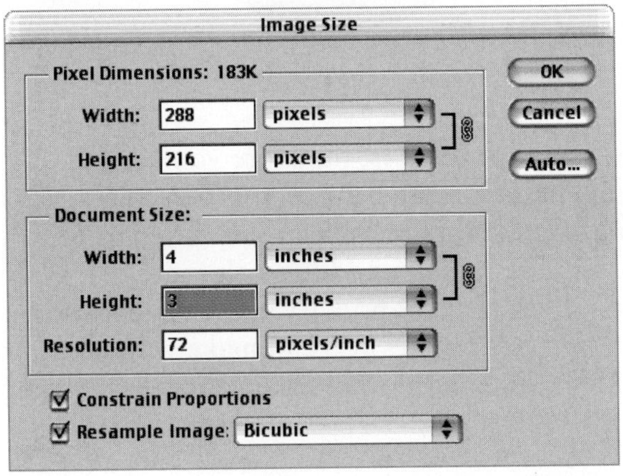

8. Save your picture and close it but leave your photo-editing software open for the next Step-By-Step.

Color

Computers are based on *additive colors*, not the *subtractive colors* you learned about in elementary school. With your crayons or poster paints, every color you colored on the page reflected less and less light—it *subtracted* light. With subtractive colors, the more you put on, the darker it gets. (Remember that ugly brown color that you would get when you accidentally put the brush in too many colors without cleaning it thoroughly?) Subtractive's primary colors are red, yellow, and blue. A basic color wheel for subtractive colors is shown in Figure 7-8.

FIGURE 7-8
Subtractive color wheel

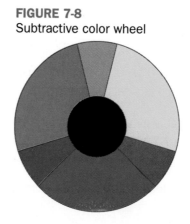

On the other hand, with additive colors, the more you add, the brighter the image becomes. With additive colors you are *adding* more light as you add colors. Because computer images are displayed by combining different colors of light, it has different primary colors (which result in different color combinations). The primary additive colors are red, green, and blue, or *RGB* as it's usually abbreviated. Table 7-1 is a chart of primary and secondary additive color mixes. These are not the same as the subtractive color mixes you can make with paint, so it might take some time to remember the combinations. Figure 7-9 shows the basic color wheel for additive colors.

TABLE 7-1
Primary and secondary additive color mixes

PRIMARY COLOR COMBINATION	SECONDARY COLOR
red + green	yellow
red + blue	magenta (bright purple)
blue + green	cyan (bright blue-green)
red + green + blue	white

FIGURE 7-9
Additive color wheel

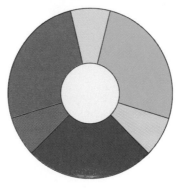

Palettes

Computers are based entirely on binary numbers. Binary refers to the way computers count—by twos. Because of this, most native computer numbers are not based on tens, but on powers of two. For example, 2^8 (two to the power of eight) is the number 256. When a picture has a ***color depth*** of 8 bits (sometimes called bit depth), only 256 different colors can be represented. The collection of 256 specific colors in a certain order is called a ***palette***. Put another way, that means that each pixel on the screen can only be one of 256 specific colors found on the palette.

The tricky part about palettes is *which* 256 colors to use. Windows has one "standard" palette of 256, and Macintosh uses another, different "standard" palette of 256 colors. To be safe, Netscape has created a third, "standard" palette of "Web-safe" colors. This palette is actually only 216 colors, with some colors leftover for each operating system. (See Appendix A for more information on Web-safe colors.)

FIGURE 7-10
The Macintosh and Windows 8-bit color palettes

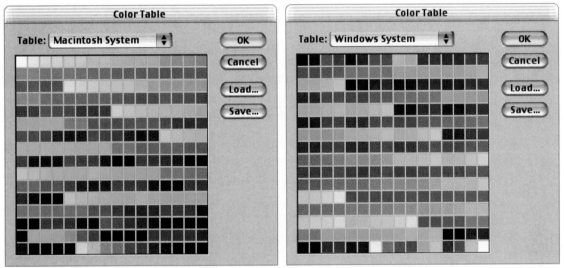

A palette of 16-bit color depth would have 2^{16} (two to the power of sixteen) colors or 65,526 different colors (called simply "thousands" of colors on the Macintosh). A 24-bit color palette would have 2^{24} (two to the power of twenty-four) or 16,777,216 colors (called simply "millions" of colors on the Macintosh). Unless you know that *all* your viewers are going to have computers with the ability to display thousands or millions of colors, it is best to use Netscape's 216 safe colors on your Web page graphics.

Making Pixels Look Good

Because of the low resolution, something that looks very clear on paper often looks somewhat jagged or blurry on a computer screen. Because pixels are square, it's very difficult to display things like curves or diagonal lines without their appearing to be like little stair steps, as in Figure 7-11. This jaggedness is called *aliasing*.

FIGURE 7-11
The letter "a" showing aliasing

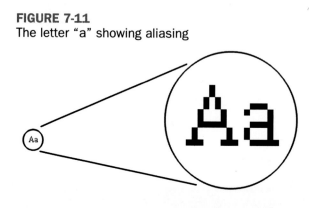

To fix this, sometimes the pixels around an object on the screen are colored with colors that are "between" the object and the background. This makes them look smoother, but a closer look makes them look blurred instead of stair-stepped (see Figure 7-12). This process of using colors to fool the eye into thinking something is smooth is called *anti-aliasing*.

FIGURE 7-12
The letter "a" showing anti-aliasing

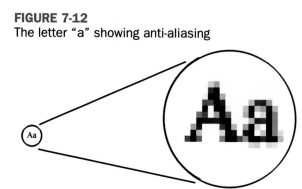

A technique very similar to anti-aliasing that can be used to make up for the small number of colors in some palettes is called *dithering*. If two dots of different colors are small enough, when your eye sees them together it will mix them together and see only one color that is "in between" the two. In other words, if you put a red pixel next to a blue pixel on a black screen, it will look like a magenta (bright purple) dot.

Computers use this to trick your eyes into seeing colors that aren't really there by scattering limited colors next to each other to give the effect of more colors. It is a way to make the 256 colors in an 8-bit color palette seem like a lot more.

Figure 7-13 shows two pictures. The one on the left is the image in full color (or as it would be seen on a computer where millions of colors are available). The one on the right is the same picture as it would be seen when only an 8-bit color palette is available but dithering is applied.

FIGURE 7-13
An enlargement of a picture of a girl with full color (left) and with dithering (right)

© Corel

Graphics Formats

There are two graphics formats common on the Web: *GIF* and *JPEG* (sometimes written JPG). To use these two formats, it is important that you know a little about them.

CompuServe's Graphic Interchange Format—GIF

GIF (which stands for Graphic Interchange Format) was developed by an online company called CompuServe to send graphics over telecommunication lines to its subscribers. A GIF has the following characteristics:

- It is compressed or made smaller to make it easy to transmit over the Web.

- It must be in 8-bit color (256 colors).

- It can appear in phases—with a low-resolution picture appearing first, then a higher resolution, then the highest. This is very appealing to Web designers because it lets the user know that a picture is coming, and roughly what it will look like very early in the download.

- It can be used to create simple animations; that is, Web designers can change pictures over time so that they appear to move. This makes the files relatively large, so GIF animations are usually created with four or five pictures that are looped (played over and over again). Animated GIFs can be real eye-catchers!

- Parts of it can be made transparent so it can be used on top of other pictures and backgrounds.

- Because it was the first inline graphic format used, it is the most compatible with older browsers.

When images are physically small in size and simple in color makeup, GIF is the best choice. Therefore, they are especially useful for small, simple graphics such as buttons, logos, icons, and other simple interface graphics.

Many graphics programs can create GIF images. Some of these programs have very few options; others provide the artist with lots of options. Consult with your instructor or technical support personnel to determine what software applications are available to you.

STEP-BY-STEP 7.3

1. Open **Step7-3.tif** in Photoshop (or in the photo-editing software you are using).

2. Click the **Image** menu and then select **Mode**. From the submenu select **Indexed Color** (see Figure 7-14).

FIGURE 7-14
The menus for changing an image to 256 colors in Photoshop

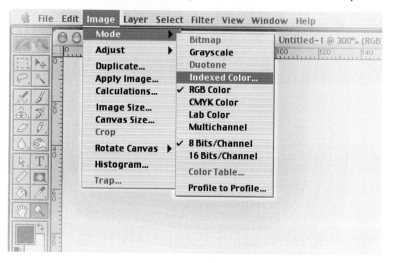

3. In the Indexed Color dialog box that opens, select **Web** from the pop-up list for Palettes (see Figure 7-15).

FIGURE 7-15
Selecting a palette for changing an image to 256 colors

4. Choose whether you want dithering or not. (Generally, if the picture is a photograph, you do.) Click on **OK** to reduce the picture to the 8-bit Web palette.

STEP-BY-STEP 7.3 Continued

5. Open the **File** menu and choose **Save As**. A dialog box similar to the one in Figure 7-16 will appear.

FIGURE 7-16
Saving your reduced-color picture in Photoshop

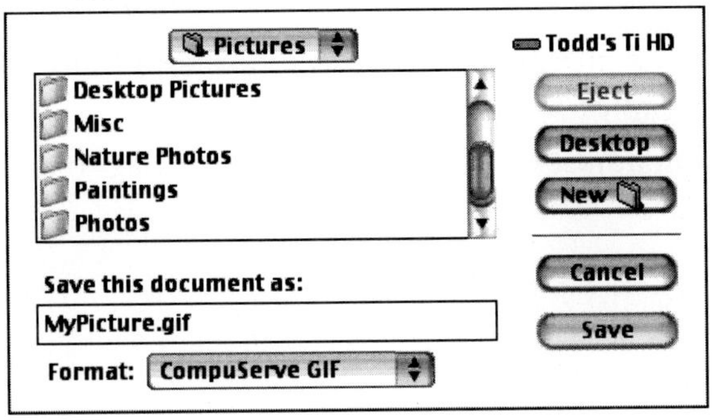

6. Use the **Format** drop-down list (like the one near the bottom of the figure) to choose the **GIF** format. (Photoshop calls it **CompuServe GIF**.)

7. If you were planning on using this graphic in a Web page, you would need to navigate to the same directory as the Web page that uses this graphic, or to a special graphics directory on your Web site. In this case, follow your instructor's directions for the location in which to save this file.

8. Key the filename **My GIF Image** into the Save this document as text box (the .gif extension will automatically be added to your filename) and click on **OK** to save it.

9. Close your image but leave your photo-editing software open for the next Step-by-Step.

JPEG—The Joint Photographer's Expert Group Format

Another common format for inline display of graphics is the JPEG format (pronounced jay-peg). JPEG was developed by the Joint Photographer's Expert Group, and the format took on the initials of the group that developed it. JPEG was not specifically developed for use on the Web, but the Web is the perfect medium for use of this format. The JPEG format has the following characteristics:

■ Because it is designed for use with photographs, 8-bit (256-color) graphics are not allowed; pictures must be in RGB format (which is one way to represent thousands of colors).

■ Unlike GIF, where there is only one level of compression, JPEG allows various compression and quality levels. Obviously, the more a picture is compressed, the less attractive it will be, and vice versa. On a scale of 1 to 10, 1 is the lowest quality with the most compression; 10 represents the highest quality with the least compression. Most people cannot tell a picture compressed at 10 from the original. A good compression level to start with is 6 or 7.

■ Another difference between this format and GIF is that there is no transparency. This means that it is often not a good choice for buttons and other screen interface elements. Also, JPEG graphics cannot be animated like GIF files.

■ This format is not particularly good at compressing physically small graphics. In fact, even though JPEG is a more sophisticated format than GIF, a small graphic compressed in both is often smaller in GIF than in JPEG. A large, complex graphic, such as a photograph, for example, is usually much better compressed using JPEG, and the result is much more attractive. For this reason JPEG is considered best for large photographs and artwork.

■ JPEG requires browsers newer than Netscape and IE version 3.

■ Most professional graphics programs (such as Adobe Photoshop) support JPEG as an option.

Next, we'll show you how to create a JPEG image. Again we are using Photoshop for our illustration. You may need to adjust the steps you take according to the software application you are using.

S TEP-BY-STEP 7.4

1. In Photoshop, open **Step7-4.tif**.

2. Select the **Image** menu, and then select **Mode**; this will open the submenu from which you should select **RGB Color**. This converts your image into the proper mode for saving in JPEG format.

3. Open the **File** menu, and select **Save As** to open the Save As dialog box.

4. Select **JPEG** from the **Format** drop-down list.

5. Key **My JPG Image.jpg** in the Save this document as text box (see Figure 7-17).

FIGURE 7-17
The Save As dialog box in Photoshop

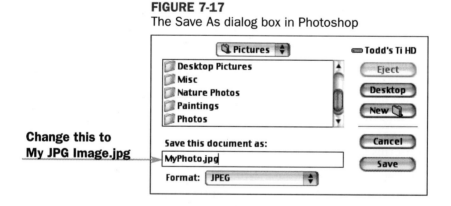

Change this to
My JPG Image.jpg

6. If you were planning on using this graphic in a Web page, you would need to navigate to the same directory as the Web page that uses this graphic, or to a special graphics directory on your Web site. In this case, follow your instructor's directions for the location in which to save this file.

7. Click **Save**. The JPEG Options dialog box opens. JPEG can save on a scale of quality levels. These levels are usually on a 10-point scale where 1 is the smallest, but least attractive, and 10 is the largest, but best-looking.

STEP-BY-STEP 7.4 Continued

8. Choose a **6** or a **7** to start with. The JPEG Options dialog box in Photoshop looks like Figure 7-18.

FIGURE 7-18
The JPEG Options dialog box in Photoshop

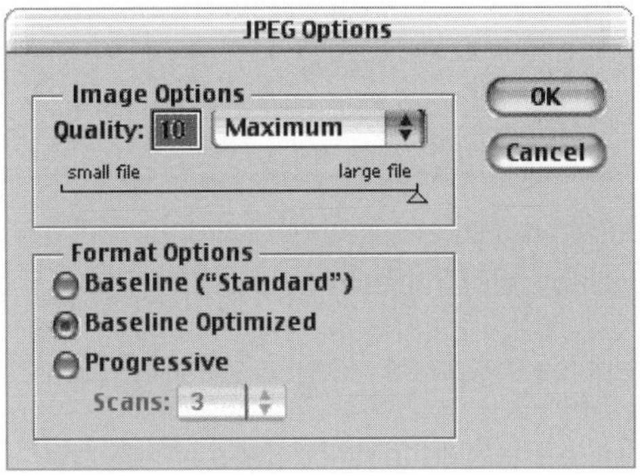

9. Click **OK** to complete the save of this image.

10. Close the file but leave your photo-editing software open for the next Step-by-Step.

Extra for Experts

Animated GIFs are fun and widely available on the Web. Use your Internet search tool to find a site that will let you download animated GIF files to use in your Web page creations.

Historically Speaking

Nearly all browsers in multitasking operating systems (like Windows and Macintosh) have the ability to use helper applications. Helper applications are opened when a file format the browser cannot display is received. The browser calls on these other applications to attempt to show the file being transmitted. This will work with nearly any kind of file (for instance, you can download a Microsoft Word document that will then automatically open Microsoft Word for you), but it is especially useful for graphic formats other than GIF and JPEG. There are "players" for nearly every format. The disadvantage to using helper applications is that these pictures will appear outside the browser window—they cannot be directly associated with the content of the page. Nor can you tell where the other window is going to be located, or what's going to happen to it when you change what's in your browser's window.

Another capability available since version 2 browsers is the ability to use plug-ins, which are small pieces of computer code that, when placed in a particular folder near the browser software, act like they are part of the browser. This feature permits plug-ins to display many other formats "inline," among other things. One of the most popular plug-ins is QuickTime from Apple Computers. QuickTime allows digital video movies to be played inline on your browser's screen. The newest version also permits a plethora of graphic formats to be displayed. Another popular plug-in is Shockwave, which allows a kind of interactive vector graphic to be displayed.

Building and Testing Graphics

Once you've created a graphic for your Web page, how can you tell if it's any good? As with anything else, you should test it. Testing graphics can be a little tricky because everyone thinks differently. So, to ensure that you get responses you can depend on, use an expert whose artistic opinion you admire. An art teacher or artistic friend is most appropriate.

STEP-BY-STEP 7.5

1. If you have not already done so, gather together or produce all the graphics that will be used in your Web site. Make these available electronically by scanning them, if needed.

2. Number or name your graphics so you can identify them in your notes.

3. Make any changes that will be needed to place them on your Web site, such as changing resolution or file format. Be sure to keep originals unchanged and work on copies so that if you accidentally make an undesired change, you will still have the original artwork from which to start.

4. Identify someone who can be a good judge of your work in graphics. An artistic classmate or colleague or an art instructor is a good choice.

5. Make an appointment to sit down with this person at a computer where you can view the electronic versions of the pictures for a sufficient amount of time to get his or her feedback. You should plan on at least three to five minutes per picture.

6. During the meeting take notes on any comments. Comments may include items such as suggestions about color, principle or elements of design, or other recommendations.

7. After your meeting, go over your notes carefully. Next to those items you can change put an asterisk (*). Next to those you might be able to change, put a letter 'm' (for "maybe"). Next to those items you definitely will not be able to change put an 'X'.

8. Make as many of the changes noted in the previous step as you can. You should make all the '*' changes, and as many of the 'm' changes as possible.

9. Save your work and then close your photo-editing software.

SUMMARY

In this lesson, you learned:

■ How graphics can become part of a Web site's message.

■ How graphics are used as interface elements.

■ How a Web site's theme can be enhanced by graphics.

■ The concepts of pixels, additive and subtractive colors, palettes, anti-aliasing, and dithering.

■ How and when to create GIF and JPEG graphics.

VOCABULARY *Review*

Define the following terms:

Additive color	Icon	Representation
Aliasing	Inline graphic	Resolution
Anti-aliasing	JPEG	RGB
Color depth	Metaphor	Subtractive color
Dithering	Palette	Symbols
GIF	Pixel	Text graphics

REVIEW *Questions*

TRUE/FALSE

Circle T if the statement is true or F if the statement is false.

T F 1. Graphics must always be part of the message of a Web page.

T F 2. Graphics can serve as part of the user interface and theme at the same time.

T F 3. Pixels are the sets of colors in which pictures can be created.

T F 4. Computer screens use subtractive color.

T F 5. Characters look smoother if they are anti-aliased.

FILL IN THE BLANK

Complete the following sentences by writing the correct word or words in the blanks provided.

1. When a graphic is a depiction of something real it is a(n) _____.

2. A(n) _____ is an abstract graphic that represents something.

3. Graphics can also serve as part of the _____, that is, the functional navigation of the Web page.

4. The trash can is an example of a graphic that is a(n) _____.

5. Small graphics with few colors, to be used as icons and such, are best stored in the _____ format.

6. Large photographic graphics are best saved in the _____ format.

WRITTEN QUESTIONS

Write a brief answer to each of the following questions.

1. How are inline graphics important to the history of the Web?

2. What conditions would justify the use of a very large graphic on a Web page?

3. When would you use GIF to store images?

4. Why might you wish to use anti-aliasing in your graphics?

5. How are computer colors different from printed colors?

PROJECTS

PROJECT 7-1

You are the contractor on a Web site project. You have just hired a new graphic artist to help you with the graphics on the Web site. She is knowledgeable about Photoshop and other tools, but she has never done Web graphics before, so she's unfamiliar with the concepts. Think about what you feel she would need to know to do her job and write your ideas in a report. The questions given below may help in organizing your thoughts.

- How are computer colors different from printed colors?

- What resolution should you use for Web-based graphics?

- What palette should you use for Web pages, and why would you use this palette?

- What are two tricks to make computer graphics seem like more than they are?

PROJECT 7-2

Continuing with the scenario begun in Project 7-1, you find, after two week's work, that your new graphic artist is saving all of her work in the GIF format. How would you explain to her the need to save at least some of her graphics in JPEG instead of GIF? Write this information in a memo. Give her a list of rules to follow for when to use each format.

PROJECT 7-3

Cut construction paper of at least three different colors into small squares. Now, carefully experiment with putting these squares together into patterns to make them appear to be different colors. Each small square is the equivalent of a pixel. Because the squares are large, you may need to paste them onto a piece of black paper and set them across the room to see the color effect. (Black paper is like the mask or screen that many color monitors use around the pixels. They use black so that the background doesn't interfere with the colors in the pixels.)

PROJECT 7-4

Your teacher will provide you four pictures in TIFF format (**Project7-4a.tif**, **Project 7-4b.tif**, **Project7-4c.tif**, and **Project7-4d.tif**). Analyze these pictures and determine which would be best put into GIF format and which would be best put into JPEG format. Then use PhotoShop or some other graphic program to modify all the graphics by reducing them to approximately 4 inches tall (or 4 inches wide for the one that is "landscape"). You may also need to reduce some to an 8-bit color palette.

TEAMWORK PROJECT

Imagine that your team is a group of judges evaluating the use of graphics in news Web sites. Find the URLs for Web pages from several News outlets (your list may include ABC News, CBS News, CNN, *The New York Times*, *Newsweek* magazine, your local newspaper, or other sources of news). Then, as a group, evaluate these Web pages' use of graphics. Identify winners in the following categories:

- Best Use of Graphics in Navigation (buttons, headings, etc.)

- Best use of bandwidth (most conservative use of graphics)

- Best use of graphics as content

- Best of Show (give a first, second, and third place award in this category)

CRITICAL *Thinking*

With what you know about Web design to this point, write a 100-word answer to one of the following questions.

SCANS ACTIVITY 7-1

What is the difference between subtractive and additive colors?

SCANS ACTIVITY 7-2

What are pixels and how can they be manipulated to display more colors than actually exist in an 8-bit color palette?

BEGINNING HTML

OBJECTIVES

Upon completion of this lesson you should be able to:

■ Explain the basic syntax of HTML.

■ Do simple markup of a text document in HTML.

■ Use document tags (HTML, HEAD, BODY, and TITLE).

■ Use formatting tags (P, BR, and HR) with some of their attributes.

■ Use text styles tags (I, B, U, and FONT) with some of their attributes.

■ Use heading and list tags for organizing the document.

■ Use the image tag (IMG) with its attributes.

■ Use the anchor tag (A) with its main attribute to link to another Web page.

■ Test your HTML documents.

Estimated time: 3.5 hours

VOCABULARY

Alpha testing

Anchor tag

Angle brackets

Attributes

Beta testing

Bullet

Document tags

Ending tag

Horizontal rule

HTML

Markup language

Metadata

Nesting

Ordered list

Sans serif

Unordered list

What Is HTML?

Markup vs. Programming

Strictly speaking, HyperText Markup Language (*HTML*) is a *markup language*, not a programming language—even though we often speak of programming a Web page in HTML. Markup language is different from a programming language in that instead of making the computer *act* a certain way, it just makes the text and other elements of the screen *display* a certain way. Markup languages allow for very little interaction with the user, while programming languages allow the user to have a lot of interaction.

With most programming languages (such as Java, C++, and Visual Basic) you begin with a text file, but that is then compiled into a machine-readable computer code file that is virtually impossible for a person to read. This machine-readable file (sometimes called a binary file) is the program or

145

application file. In a markup language, a simple text file contains both the content and the markup, and it remains a text file—so a person can easily read it, even after it is marked up.

HTML Markup Syntax

To mark up files, you insert little tags into the body of the text that tell the computer's browser how to display the text. The tags have to be a little different from regular text so that the browser knows that they are tags and not just part of the text. In HTML you use the less than sign (<) and the greater than sign (>) as brackets around the tags to identify them. We call these *angle brackets*. A pair of these around some text tells the browser to do something with the information between them. If the information between the brackets doesn't make sense to the browser, the browser will just ignore the information. Figure 8-1 is an example of the bold tag in HTML.

FIGURE 8-1
The bold tag created with angle brackets

```
<B>
```

In addition to having angle brackets around the tag, you sometimes want to turn something on in the text and then turn it off again. For example, the tag above turns on bold. That means that everything after this tag will be in boldface. How do you turn bold off? You need an *ending tag*. The ending tag usually repeats the command but begins with a forward slash, as shown in Figure 8-2.

> **Note** ☑
>
> In this lesson we will key all markup tags in CAPITAL LETTERS to make them easy to see. In practice, with most browsers, it doesn't matter whether the markup tags are capital or lowercase letters.

FIGURE 8-2
The ending bold tag created by adding a forward slash

```
</B>
```

Use these tags together in an HTML document to turn boldface on and off. Figure 8-3 shows a pair of bold tags used to make one word in a sentence bold.

FIGURE 8-3
The bold tag in use

```
<B> Giraffes <B> are known for their long necks
```

In this example, the word giraffes is in boldface; all the rest of the text is in a normal type, as shown in Figure 8-4.

FIGURE 8-4
The HTML text from Figure 8-3 as it would appear

Giraffes are known for their long necks.

Notice that tags have disappeared, but the word giraffes is in boldface type.

Some tags do not need an ending tag; some tags require an ending tag. For others, an ending tag is optional. Figure 8-5 shows a tag that does not need an ending tag. It draws a horizontal line (called a *Horizontal Rule* or HR for short) across the screen.

FIGURE 8-5
The Horizontal Rule tag doesn't need an ending tag

```
<HR>
```

You can see that an ending tag in this case doesn't make a lot of sense. There is no need to tell it to stop drawing the Horizontal Rule because it just draws one line anyway. (You could use an ending tag, </HR>, but because this is nonsense to the browser, it will just ignore it. Besides, what text would it go around? There is nothing to put between these tags.)

Nesting Tags

Another characteristic of tags is that sets of tags can be placed inside of other tags. For example, if you wanted a word to be both bold and italic you could surround it with a pair of bold tags and then surround all that with a pair of italics tags. This is called *nesting*. Figure 8-6 shows how correctly nested tags should look.

FIGURE 8-6
Nested tags

```
A <I><B>giraffe</B></I> is a long-necked animal related to deer.
```

These nested tags would make the text appear in a browser as it is shown in Figure 8-7.

FIGURE 8-7
The HTML text from Figure 8-6 shown in a browser

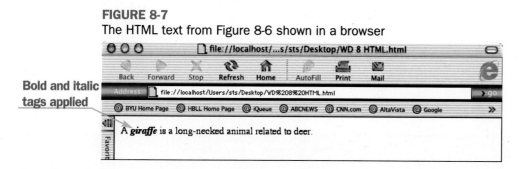

Bold and italic
tags applied

The only trick to nesting is that you should always back out of the tags in the reverse order that you went into them. For example, if you first turned on italics and then boldface, you should turn off boldface before turning off italics.

A way to remember this is to draw a line between each opening and closing tag. If the lines cross, they are nested incorrectly (see Figure 8-8).

FIGURE 8-8
Inappropriately nested tags (notice the crossed lines) and appropriately nested tags

Wrong

A\<B>\<I>Giraffe\</B>\</I> is a long-necked animal related to deer.

Right

A\<B>\<I>Giraffe\</I>\</B> is a long-necked animal related to deer.

Attributes

Sometimes it is possible for a tag to be implemented in more than one way. When this is the case, you can usually add an *attribute* to the tag to tell the browser exactly how to implement it. Attributes are found inside the angle brackets of the opening tag. For example, in the \<HR> tag above, you may elect to have a thicker line than the default two-pixel line it usually creates. When this is the case you can add a size attribute and change the thickness of the line, as shown in Figure 8-9.

FIGURE 8-9
The Horizontal Rule tag with an attribute

```
<HR size="7">
```

Internet Milestone

XML

One of the weaknesses of HTML is that it is a limited set of specific tags. What if you want to do something completely different? What if you want to make up your own tags to do special things? Something relatively new that will provide the ability to do just that is called "XML," which stands for eXtensible Markup Language. An XML document is combined with a style sheet that tells the receiving browser what to do with the XML tags.

This tag will draw a horizontal rule (line) that is seven pixels thick, as shown in Figure 8-10.

FIGURE 8-10
The HTML tag from Figure 8-9 shown in a browser

Note that ending tags do not have attributes. Attributes are only found in the opening tag of the tag set.

STEP-BY-STEP 8.1

1. Figure 8-11 is a part of an HTML document with some errors in it. Find all the errors and rewrite the document correcting them.

FIGURE 8-11
An HTML document with errors

<H1>Creating Web Pages
<P>There are many wonderful tools for creating Web pages. Many of these tools are <B><I>WYSI WYG</B></I> — "what you see is what you get." When you use these tools you actually see what your Web page will look like as you create it. However you don't need fancy tools to create Web pages. All you need is a simple text editor and a browser.</P>
<P>To create Web pages, you can use the simple text editor that came with your computer: <I>SimpleText</I> or <I>TextEdit on the Macintosh and <I>Notepad</I> or <I>WordPad on the PC. You can key text and markup commands directly into a plain old text document. (You can also use a word processor such as <I>Microsoft Word</I> or <I>Corel WordPerfect<I>, but if you do, be sure to save the document as a plain text file.)
<P>After you have created a document, you need to save it with the extension <B><I>.html</B><I> or <I><B>.htm</B></I>. Adding this extension to the filename tells both the browser and the operating system that the document is an HTML browser document.</P>
<P>Once you have saved it, you can open it in your browser. After you have looked at it in the browser, you will, no doubt, want to make changes. To do so, you simply return to the text editor, make your changes, save the document, and open it again in the browser. Even easier: Most browsers have a <B>refresh<B> button. If yours has one, you don't even need to reopen the text document. After you've opened the document into the window the first time, you can simply click the refresh button and the most recently saved version of the HTML document will appear in the browser window.<P>

STEP-BY-STEP 8.1 Continued

FIGURE 8-11 Continued
An HTML document with errors

<P>Unlike most programs, you can have the text file open in <I>both</B> the text editor and in the browser. This is because the browser cannot change the document; it can only show it. When an application can only read a document, the operating system allows the document to be open in more than one place at a time. This fact will allow you to make changes quickly and view them as you build your HTML document.</P>

2. Your instructor has the correct answer. Compare your corrected document with the correct text.

3. Make any additional changes you may have missed.

4. Optional: The surest way to test an HTML document is to key it into a text editor and view it in a browser. To ensure that you caught all the errors, key this text with its tags, save it, and view it in the browser.

Document Tags

There is a set of tags that is used to surround the entire document and various parts of the document. Because these tags are used on the whole Web page, we call them *document tags*. At a minimum, every page should have these document tags. Other tags are then added as needed.

HTML Tag

The HTML tag (<HTML>) should be used at the very beginning of the document, and its closing tag (</HTML>) should be placed at the very end of the document. Some browsers use this tag to determine how to interpret the document. This tag signals to the browser that the document can be displayed as HTML text.

HEAD and BODY Tags

Once you have used the <HTML> tag to identify the document, you will want to use the <HEAD> and <BODY> tags to separate the document into two parts, a head and a body.

The head (that material inside the <HEAD> tags) will not be visible to the user, except for the title (see below). However, this space can be used to insert information about the Web pages that will help users find your page, such as indexing words called *metadata*. When search engines are classifying pages, they often use metadata to help them recognize what the Web page is about.

The <BODY> tags surround the part of your Web page that is visible to the public in the browser window. Put another way, most of the content of your Web pages will be inside the <BODY> tags (which are inside the <HTML> tags).

The <BODY> tag is one of those tags that can have attributes. One of the <BODY> tag's attributes can change the background color of the page (bgcolor, which you can set to any standard color name). Another attribute can set up an image to be a background image (background). These attributes are shown in Figure 8-12.

FIGURE 8-12
Two attributes for the BODY tag: background color and background image

```
<BODY bgcolor="blue">
or
<BODY background="myBackgroundImage.jpg">
```

In the first example, the background color is set to the color blue. In the second, a JPEG image called *myBackgroundImage.jpg* is used as the background of the Web page.

TITLE Tag

The <TITLE> tag goes in the <HEAD> of the document. The text between the <TITLE> tags will appear as the title of the browser window in most browsers. A typical <TITLE> tag and text is shown in Figure 8-13.

FIGURE 8-13
Using the TITLE tag

```
<HEAD>
<TITLE>Animals of the Serengeti</TITLE>
</HEAD>
```

This tag, when placed in the head of a Web page, will appear in a browser as shown in Figure 8-14.

FIGURE 8-14
The HTML title text from Figure 8-13 shown in a browser's title bar

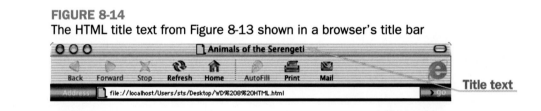

Title text

S TEP-BY-STEP 8.2

In all the remaining Step-by-Steps of this lesson, you will be creating a Web page about animals of the Serengeti Plain in Africa.

1. Using SimpleText (on a Macintosh) or Notepad (on a PC), open a new text document.

STEP-BY-STEP 8.2 Continued

2. Key the sets of tags shown in Figure 8-15. (We have indented the text to illustrate the nesting—your document does not have to show these indents.)

FIGURE 8-15
Typical document tags with which to start a Web page

```
<HTML>
<HEAD>
</HEAD>
<BODY>

</BODY>
</HTML>
```

3. Save your document as **animals.html**.

4. Between the <HEAD> tags, insert the following text: **<TITLE>Animals of the Serengeti</TITLE>**. Your document will look something like Figure 8-16.

> **Note** ☑
>
> Some applications may not allow you to save your document with the .html extension. If yours is one of these, view the file from the operating system's directory and rename it to have an .html or .htm ending.

FIGURE 8-16
Typical document tags with a TITLE tag

```
<HTML>
<HEAD>
<TITLE>Animals of the Serengeti</TITLE>
</HEAD>
<BODY>

</BODY>
</HTML>
```

5. Save your document again.

6. If it is not already open, open your browser.

7. In the browser, click the **File** menu and select the option for opening a file.

8. Navigate to your new text file (*animals.html*) and open it in the browser. Note that you have not yet added any content, so you will see only a blank browser window. However, you will see the title at the top of the window, as shown in Figure 8-17.

STEP-BY-STEP 8.2 Continued

9. Leave both the browser window and the text editor open for the next Step-by-Step.

FIGURE 8-17
The HTML tags and text from Figure 8-16 as seen in a browser

Title text

file://localhost/Users/sts/Desktop/WD%208%20HTML.html

Formatting Tags

P (Paragraph) Tag

The paragraph tag (<P>) is probably the most common tag in all HTML documents. This is because it is used between every paragraph in all the Web pages on the Web.

The ending paragraph tag (</P>) is optional, but we encourage you to use ending paragraph tags so that you can take advantage of some of the special features of the paragraph tag. For example, you can use the paragraph tag to center text by putting an "align="center"" attribute in it.

For example, Figure 8-18 shows how the first line of a famous poem by William Blake would be marked up if you wanted it to be its own paragraph and centered on the page.

FIGURE 8-18
Use of the paragraph tag with the align attribute

```
<P align="center">Tyger, tyger, burning bright,</P>
```

Programming Skills

WYSIWYG HTML EDITORS

You probably recognized early on that this was harder than it needed to be—and you're right. There are several good WYSIWYG HTML editors that can help you create high-quality HTML without ever looking at a text editor. So why are we making you learn HTML the hard way? Because with this little bit of skill, you can "look under the hood" of the HTML code that those editors create when you need to fix something. Understanding how tags work will ultimately make you a much better HTML programmer, no matter what tool you use.

This text will look like Figure 8-19 when it is viewed in a browser.

FIGURE 8-19
The HTML text from Figure 8-18 when viewed in a browser

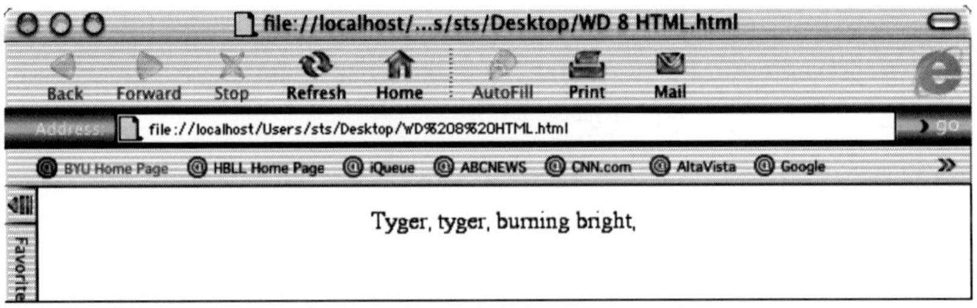

BR (Break) Tag

The break tag (<BR>) is probably the next-most-common tag in HTML after the paragraph tag. The difference between the break tag and the paragraph tag is that the paragraph tag is like putting two returns between paragraphs. The break tag is like putting a single return after a line. If you want to separate two paragraphs with a blank white space between them, use a paragraph tag. However, if you want to just break to the next line, use a break tag.

Because the break tag does not contain any text, it does not have an ending tag. (Of course you can put one in, but the browser will ignore it.)

In the poem that we began as an example for the paragraph tag, we don't want white space between each line—we just want a line break. So now we will add another line to the poem, but we will keep it in the same paragraph by using the break tag. To do this we mark up our text as shown in Figure 8-20.

FIGURE 8-20
Using the break tag to add a new line to a paragraph

```
<P align="center">Tyger, tyger, burning bright,<BR>In the jungles of the night</P>
```

This will result in text that, when seen in a browser, looks like Figure 8-21.

FIGURE 8-21
The HTML text from Figure 8-20 as it appears in a browser

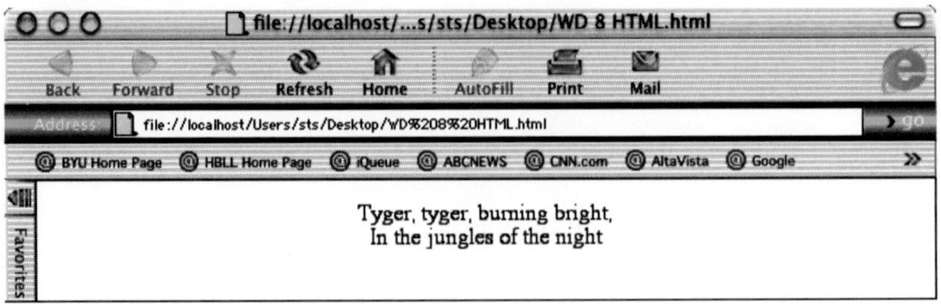

Notice that it didn't matter that you did not put a return between the lines in the HTML document—it still displayed correctly. This is another important fact about HTML. The returns and extra spaces in the document are ignored. All the browser pays attention to are the tags. The text displayed in the browser would look exactly the same, even if you keyed it as shown in Figure 8-22.

FIGURE 8-22
Arrangement of text that has the same result as the text in Figure 8-20

```
<P align="center">Tyger,
tyger,
burning

bright,
<BR>
In the
jungles
of the
night</P>
```

The extra returns are basically ignored (actually, they're treated like single spaces). If you viewed this text in the browser it would appear identical to that shown in Figure 8-21.

HR (Horizontal Rule) Tag

The Horizontal Rule (<HR>) is a tag that draws a line between paragraphs. The word rule in this case is related to the word ruler and is printer terminology for a straight line. You've already seen this tag in use.

This tag separates what is above it from what is below it with a line. Attributes can control the width of the line (width=) and how thick it is (size=) in pixels. For example, suppose we wanted a line above the poem that was equal to 50% of the width of the browser window and five pixels thick. To do this you would put the tag shown in Figure 8-23 above the poem.

FIGURE 8-23
The Horizontal Rule tag with width and size attributes

```
<HR width="50%" size="5">
```

When viewed in a browser, the tag shown in Figure 8-23 would appear as shown in Figure 8-24.

FIGURE 8-24
The HTML tag from Figure 8-23 as seen in a browser

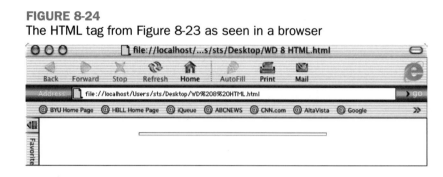

STEP-BY-STEP 8.3

1. If it is not already open, open the **animals.html** document in your text editor, or if the browser is in front of it, switch to the text editor.

2. Click in the blank space between the <BODY> tags, and insert the text shown in Figure 8-25.

> **Note** ☑
> Your instructor has access to the text found in Figure 8-25 and may choose to supply it to you rather than having you key it.

FIGURE 8-25
Text for Step-by-Step 8.3

Lions
Probably the most famous creatures to live in the Serengeti are the lions. Male lions are known for their manes, the bushy growth of hair that surrounds their faces. The mane makes them look larger and more ferocious than they really are. But, in fact, the females are the more active and adept hunters.

Lions travel in groups called prides. A pride consists of one leader male, several lesser males, and a group of females and their offspring. Lions are meat-eaters and can go days without eating and then gorge themselves on a killed antelope or another animal.

Giraffes
Giraffes are known for their long necks. Their long necks help them eat the leaves near the tops of trees. Giraffes have long lips with which they pull leaves from the trees to eat. Surprisingly, they have no more bones in their neck than a mouse!

Less famous is the beautiful webbed pattern on their fur, which is striking up close, but actually helps camouflage them from a distance. It is also fun to watch them run, because their long limbs make them so graceful.

Hyenas
Hyenas are related to dogs and have a lot of the same behaviors: They travel and hunt in packs. In fact a single hyena is not nearly as dangerous as a pack of them. In a pack, different hyenas perform different roles, like a football team. In this way they can take down much larger animals, such as musk ox and lions. Hyenas and lions are natural enemies because they eat the same foods. Often hyenas will scavenge an abandoned lion's kill.

Hyenas are sometimes called laughing hyenas, but it's just because the call of one breed is reminiscent of our laughing. In reality, there is nothing funny about hyenas.

STEP-BY-STEP 8.3 Continued

3. Surround each of the paragraphs with **<P>** tags. For the time being, treat the headings like paragraphs, with their own <P> tags.

4. Separate each of the three animal names and descriptions with **<HR>** tags.

5. Save your work.

6. View your text in the browser to see what it looks like. Leave both the browser and the text editor open for the next Step-by-Step.

Text Style Tags

Some tags can be used to make the text itself look different, either through making it italic (slanted), boldface, or underlined. Other tags can change the actual style of the text—or the font—that is to be used.

> **Net Tip**
>
> We do not recommend using the underline tag since it may make your text look like a hyperlink. It is generally recommended that you use italics to emphasize text instead of the underline.

I (Italics) Tag, B (Bold) Tag, and U (Underline) Tag

The italics tag (<I>) makes the text between the opening and closing tag italics. A bold tag (<B>), as discussed earlier in this lesson, makes the text between opening and closing boldface. And the underline tag (<U>) underlines the text.

Figure 8-26 shows how these three tags could all be used in a line of text.

FIGURE 8-26
All three text style tags used together

> This text demonstrates what <I>italics</I>, <B>boldface</B>, and <U>underlined</U> text looks like. In fact, you can do <I><B><U>all three</U></B></I>, if you want to!

Figure 8-27 shows what the HTML text shown in Figure 8-26 would look like in a browser.

FIGURE 8-27
The HTML text from Figure 8-26 as it appears in a browser

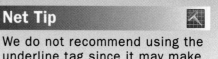

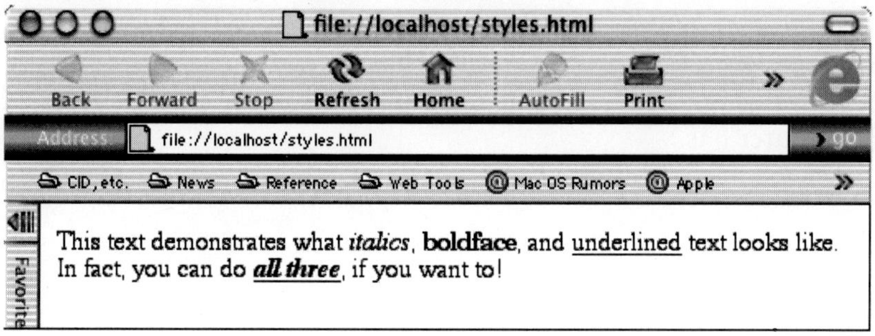

This text demonstrates what *italics*, **boldface**, and underlined text looks like. In fact, you can do ***all three***, if you want to!

The FONT Tag

In the early history of the Web, you had no choice as to which fonts you could use. Eventually, designers demanded more flexibility, so the <FONT> tag was invented. Using attributes you can select fonts to use. You are still somewhat limited since the receiving computer may not have the exact fonts you want—but it's a lot better situation than what was originally the case. Keep in mind that this tag does not *transmit* fonts; it only uses fonts that are already available on the user's system.

The <FONT> tag has several attributes, but we'll discuss only two of them here. They are *face* and *color*.

The face attribute allows you to select a font face. As with other attributes you do this with an equal sign, as shown in Figure 8-28.

FIGURE 8-28
The FONT tag used to select the font Arial

```
<FONT face="Arial">
```

However, many Macintosh computers do not have Arial on them. So for them, you will want a font that is like Arial, such as Helvetica. Simply add it to the font list, separated from Arial by a comma, as shown in Figure 8-29.

FIGURE 8-29
Using the FONT tag to select Arial if available, or Helvetica if Arial is not available on the user's computer

```
<FONT face="Arial, Helvetica">
```

On the off chance that a person visiting your Web page has neither Arial nor Helvetica, we are going to add a third font attribute that specifies only the characteristic of being *sans serif* (which means the font doesn't have those little fancy marks at the edges of each letter; both Arial and Helvetica are sans serif fonts). Figure 8-30 shows how the font tag would be written to allow for these choices.

FIGURE 8-30
The FONT tag configured to pick Arial, Helvetica, or some other sans serif font

```
<FONT face="Arial, Helvetica, sans serif">
```

Any text between this tag and its ending tag will be displayed in whichever of the three fonts listed the user's computer has.

Color works in a similar manner. To add a second attribute inside the font tag, you have to separate them with a space. For example, if we want the text to be green as well, we add a space and then the color attribute, as shown in Figure 8-31.

FIGURE 8-31
Using the FONT tag to change text color

```
<FONT face="Arial, Helvetica, sans serif" color="green">Sample Text</FONT>
```

The resulting text from the HTML text shown in Figure 8-31 will look like Figure 8-32 in a browser.

FIGURE 8-32
The HTML text from Figure 8-31 as it appears in a browser

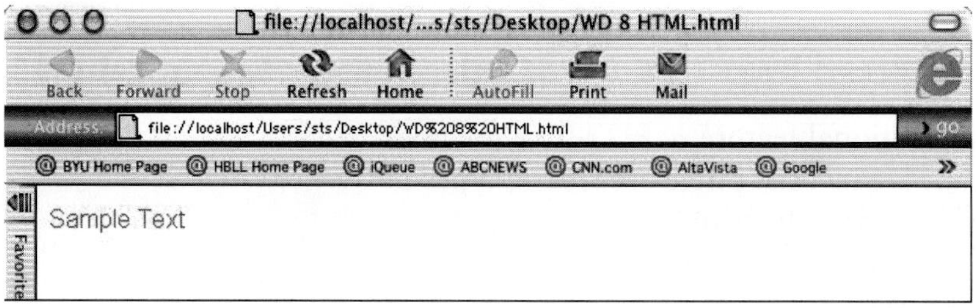

STEP-BY-STEP 8.4

1. If it is not already open, open your **animals.html** document in your text editor, or bring the text editor to the front if the browser is covering it.

2. Put **<B>** tags around each of the three titles (Lions, Giraffes, Hyenas). We're going to change these in the next Step-by-Step, but for now it will give them the effect of headings.

3. Put **<I>** tags around each of the names of the animals as it appears in the paragraphs.

4. Surround each of the paragraphs (not the headings!) with **<FONT>** tags to turn the paragraphs into blue, Arial, Helvetica, or sans serif text.

5. Save your work, and then view it in the browser to see what it looks like. Leave both the browser and the text editor open for the next Step-by-Step.

Tags for Organizing and Lists

When HTML was originally invented, its creators thought that it would be used primarily for transmitting documents such as scholarly papers. To accommodate that purpose, it has several features for organizing text such as headings and lists.

H (Heading) Tag

Documents can often be organized in an outline, with higher-level headings and lower-level headings. HTML works with this organization method by having six levels of headings. Heading level 1 is the main, top heading. The next level (level 2) is a subheading. The next (level 3) is a sub-subheading, and so forth.

Heading tags are simply the letter H (for heading) and a number, as shown in Figure 8-33.

FIGURE 8-33
A heading level 3 tag

```
<H3>Breeds of Zebras</H3>
```

This makes the phrase "Breeds of Zebras" into a level 3 heading.

Lists: UL (Unordered List) Tag, OL (Ordered List) Tag, and LI (List Item) Tag

Another organizational feature of HTML is the ability to automatically create lists. There are several types of lists, but we will discuss only two: ordered (<OL>) and unordered lists (<UL>). Lists have two components: the list tag (either <OL> or <UL>), and the tag (<LI>) for each item in the list.

For an *ordered list* (sometimes referred to as a numbered list), you surround all the list items with the <OL> tag and each item within the list with the <LI> tag, as shown in Figure 8-34.

> **Note** ☑
>
> You do not have to insert any hard returns in your HTML text when you create a list. We inserted it here to make it easier to read, but the text will be displayed the same in the browser regardless of the spacing in the original text file.

FIGURE 8-34
HTML tags for creating an ordered list

```
<OL>
<LI>Lions</LI>
<LI>Tigers</LI>
<LI>Bears</LI>
<LI>(Oh, my!)</LI>
</OL>
```

Notice that we did not include any numbers in the text of this list. In spite of that, when it is displayed in a browser, it will appear as shown in Figure 8-35.

FIGURE 8-35
The HTML text from Figure 8-34 as seen in a browser

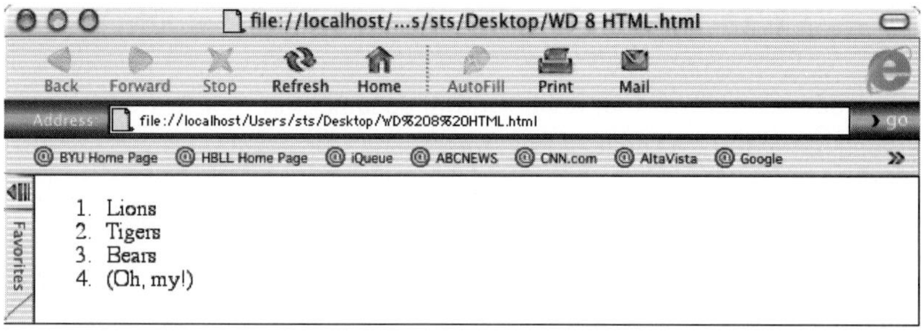

Notice that the <OL> tag does two things for you: It automatically numbers the list and it indents the items in the list. That means that the items are numbered in the order in which you place them. If you change the order, the numbering will change automatically as well.

The other type of list we will discuss is the ***unordered list*** (sometimes referred to as a ***bullet*** list). The syntax is identical to an ordered list, but the outcome is just a little different. Figure 8-36 is the same as the previous list but using <UL> instead of <OL> tags.

FIGURE 8-36
HTML tags for creating an unordered list

```
<UL>
<LI>Lions</LI>
<LI>Tigers</LI>
<LI>Bears</LI>
<LI>(Oh, my!)</LI>
</UL>
```

Notice that we did not include any bullets in the text, but when it is displayed in a browser, it appears as shown in Figure 8-37.

FIGURE 8-37
The HTML text from Figure 8-36 as it appears in a browser

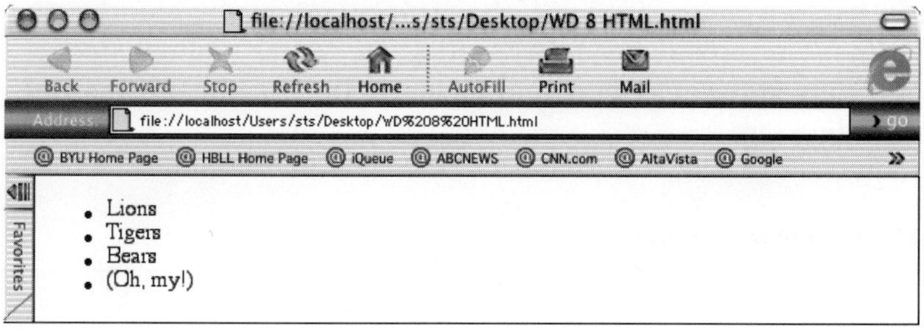

The <UL> tag indents like the <OL> tag, except the list items are preceded by bullets instead of numbers. (A bullet is a round, black dot or some other symbol used to emphasize the different elements in a list.)

STEP-BY-STEP 8.5

1. If it is not already open, open your **animals.html** document in your text editor, or if the browser is in the foreground, bring the text editor to the foreground.

2. Key **Animals of the Serengeti** at the beginning of the document.

3. Surround the text with heading 1 (**<H1>**) tags.

4. Clearly, the names of the animals at the beginning of each section of our Web page are headings. Tag them as such using **<H2>** (you may remove the <B> tags from them now that they have heading tags around them).

5. Before the first section, insert a brief table of contents listing the three sections of the page (Lions, Giraffes, and Hyenas) in either an ordered list (using **<OL>** and **<LI>** tags) or an unordered list (using **<UL>** and **<LI>** tags).

6. Save your work and view it in the browser to see what it looks like. Leave both the browser and the text editor open for the next Step-by-Step.

Tags to Insert Images

IMG (Image) Tag

If any single thing propelled the World Wide Web into a popular medium, it was the addition of pictures—right in the browser window! It doesn't seem like much to us now, but it was a really big deal then.

How do you get the pictures into the file? It's simple, really. You link a file that contains the picture to your Web page. The file must be one of two types that can be played "in line" (in the browser window): JPEG or GIF. For details on these two file format types, see Lesson 7.

Because the image has its own filename, the <IMG> tag must have at least one attribute that contains the filename. This attribute is referred to as the source (abbreviated src). The image tag with its source attribute appears as shown in Figure 8-38. For obvious reasons, the <IMG> tag does not have an ending tag.

FIGURE 8-38
The image tag with the source attribute

```
<IMG src="crocodile.jpg">
```

When viewed in a browser, this HTML tag places the named image in the location of the tag, as shown in Figure 8-39.

FIGURE 8-39
The HTML tag from Figure 8-38 as seen in a browser

Placement

An interesting set of attributes will allow you to align the picture in relation to the surrounding text. It works as shown in Figure 8-40.

FIGURE 8-40
Adding an align attribute to the image tag

```
<IMG src="SomeImage.jpg" align="right">
```

The tag shown in Figure 8-40 would align the picture to the right of the text. You will want to experiment with this attribute to learn exactly how it works—the results, at times, can be a little unexpected.

S TEP-BY-STEP 8.6

1. If it is not already open, open your **animals.html** document in your text editor, or bring the text editor to the foreground if it is behind the browser.

2. Using the <IMG> tag, add a picture of lions, a giraffe, and a hyena just before the text of each animal. (These images can be found in your data files and are named **Step8-6_Lions.jpg**, **Step8-6_Giraffe.jpg**, and **Step8-6_Hyena.jpg**.)

3. For variety's sake, align the picture of the lions on the left, the giraffe on the right, and the hyena back on the left.

4. Save your work and view it in the browser to see what it looks like.

5. Since using the align attribute takes some experimentation, change your tags to see how they turn out.

6. After each edit, save your file, then view it in the browser to see the effect of your experiments.

7. When you are satisfied with your page, save your work. Leave the browser and the text editor open for the next Step-by-Step.

Programming Skills

EMBEDDING (FLASH AND QUICKTIME)

Pictures aren't the only things that can be embedded in a Web page. You can also put movies and interactive programs into your Web pages. QuickTime movies allow high-quality video to be downloaded and played on your browser. Flash creates fascinating animated graphic programs that can also be loaded.

Tags for HyperLinks

A (Anchor) Tags

The real reason the Web was invented was so that you could do exactly what this tag allows you to do—link from one document to another. The tag that allows this is called an *Anchor tag*. It works by letting you insert an attribute that gives the address of another page to load. When an anchor tag of this type surrounds text, it is, by default, underlined and colored to help you identify it as a link.

The tag is simply <A> (for anchor). The attribute that makes it work is href, which stands for hyperreference. An anchor tag that would take you to Yahoo! would be written as shown in Figure 8-41.

FIGURE 8-41
An anchor tag

<A href="http://www.yahoo.com">Click here to go to Yahoo!</A>

The anchor tag and text written in Figure 8-41 would look like Figure 8-42 in a browser.

FIGURE 8-42
The HTML tag from Figure 8-41 as seen in a browser

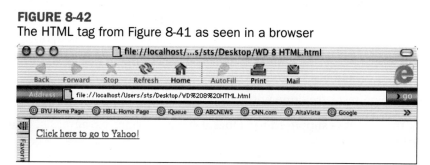

The attribute must contain a legitimate URL (such as the URL for Yahoo! above), but it does not have to be a complete URL. If the document the anchor tag is linking to is on the same computer you can do what is called a relative link. For example, suppose you have an HTML page called Me.html and you have a separate page in the same directory of your server called Friends.html to which you wanted to link. Figure 8-43 shows what your anchor tag <A> could look like.

FIGURE 8-43
HTML anchor tag for making a link to a page about friends in the same directory

<A href="Friends.html">Click here to see some of my friends</A>

Clicking on any of the text within the anchor would open up that page in your browser.

S TEP-BY-STEP 8.7

1. If it is not already open, open your **animals.html** document in your text editor, or if the browser is in the foreground, bring the text editor to the foreground.

2. At the bottom of the page, create a new paragraph (with the **<P>** tag) and insert the following information: **A Web site dedicated to the Serengeti can be found by clicking here**.

3. Around the word *here* add an anchor **<A>** tag. For the href, use the following URL: **http://www.serengeti.org**.

4. Save your work and view it in the browser to see what it looks like. Leave both the browser and the text editor open for the next Step-by-Step.

Testing Your HTML

Professional programmers do two kinds of testing: alpha and beta. *Alpha testing* is the first testing that software goes through, usually by the programmers themselves. Alpha testing involves testing all the obvious things.

Beta testing is a little more work. Someone other than the programmer tests every possible thing the computer can do. The attitude of most beta testers is to try to "break" the software. This may sound obtuse, but it is very important that this happen to guarantee that the software works.

You can alpha test your own software, but you need someone else to test everything in your Web page to complete a beta test of your Web site.

Both alpha and beta tests are done with checklists. Following is a sample checklist to use.

- Does it look the way it is supposed to? Does it have the right paragraphs, headings, lists, and so forth?

- Are all the links properly identified?

- Do all the links work? Do they go to the right places?

Programming Skills

JAVASCRIPT

Early in this lesson we said that HTML was not a programming language. In a strict sense that is true: HTML's programming ability is limited. However, noting this weakness, programming ability has been added. It is called JavaScript. If you are interested in making Web pages more interactive, we recommend a good JavaScript guide such as *HTML and JavaScript BASICS* by Barksdale and Turner.

S TEP-BY-STEP 8.8

1. Use the preceding checklist on the HTML page you created in the previous Step-by-Step exercises in this lesson.

2. Make any changes that you think are necessary, and then save and close your **animals.html** file.

3. Use the same checklist on the Web site you created for the rest of this book.

4. Make any changes that you think are necessary, and then save and retest your work.

5. Ask a knowledgeable friend (such as a classmate) to go through the checklist again on your Web site.

6. Make changes suggested by your tester, then save and view your edits.

7. When you are satisfied with the edits you have made, save your changes and then close both the browser and the text editor.

SUMMARY

In this lesson, you learned:

- To explain the basic syntax of HTML.
- How to do simple markup of a text document in HTML.
- To use document tags (HTML, HEAD, BODY, and TITLE).
- To use formatting tags (P, BR, and HR) with some of their attributes.
- To use text styles tags (I, B, U, and FONT) with some of their attributes.
- To use heading and listing tags for organizing the document.
- To use the image tag (IMG) with its attributes.
- To use the anchor tag (A) with its main attribute to link to another Web page.
- How to test your HTML documents.

VOCABULARY *Review*

Define the following terms:

Alpha testing	Document tags	Nesting
Anchor	Ending tag	Ordered list
Angle brackets	Horizontal rule	Sans serif
Attributes	HTML	Unordered list
Beta testing	Markup language	
Bullet	Metadata	

REVIEW *Questions*

TRUE/FALSE

Circle T if the statement is true or F if the statement is false.

T   F   1. HTML is a programming language.

T   F   2. HTML's codes are called tags.

T   F   3. HTML's codes are surrounded by square brackets.

T   F   4. All HTML codes require end codes.

T   F   5. Some HTML codes can have attributes added to them.

FILL IN THE BLANK

Complete the following sentences by writing the correct word or words in the blanks provided.

1. HTML stands for _____ .

2. When multiple tags are used on the same text, you have to make sure they are _____ correctly.

3. _____ , which can change how the tag works, appear only in the opening tag.

4. _____ tags are used to organize an entire document.

5. When you use a TITLE tag, the title appears in the _____ of the browser.

WRITTEN QUESTIONS

Write a brief answer to each of the following questions.

1. What tags would you use to mark up a poem so it is centered?

2. What tag would you use to separate parts of a Web page with a line?

3. What tags would you use to create a list of steps to be performed in order?

4. What tags would you use to make a link to another Web site?

5. What tag would you use to insert a picture into your Web page?

PROJECTS

PROJECT 8-1

Paula Presidente runs a nonprofit organization to help find homes for lost pets. Knowing what you know now, what services could you offer Paula to help her design, develop, and build a Web site? Put your answer in the form of a paragraph that might be part of a proposal to Paula.

PROJECT 8-2

Create a Web page that contains the information shown in Figure 8-44.

FIGURE 8-44
Text for Project 8-2 Web page

> **Other Tags: Tables, Frame Sets, Definitions Lists**
> What you are experiencing here is only a sampling of HTML tags and programming. There are lots more! For example, you can divide the browser window into smaller windows using FRAMESET tags, and you can create TABLES for placing data in columns and rows. There are also other kinds of lists than the ones we've shown you, and new ways to format the text. We recommend a good HTML guide like HTML BASICS by Barksdale and Turner.
> Following is a list of the tags you've learned:
> HTML
> HEAD
> BODY
> TITLE
> I(talics)
> B(old)
> P(aragraph)
> BR(eak)
> H(orizontal)R(ule)
> FONT
> H(eading Tags)
> O(rdered)L(ist)
> U(nordered)L(ist)
> L(ist) I(tem)
> IM(a)G(e)
> A(nchor)

TEAMWORK PROJECT

One reason people's understanding of HTML has spread so quickly is because anyone can view the HTML markup of Web pages and borrow ideas from them. (To view the HTML of a Web page in Internet Explorer, select Source from the View menu.) Have each member of your team find a Web page that he or she likes. Then look at the source of that page to try to discover a new HTML markup tag or a new way to use one of the HTML tags you learned in this lesson. Then have each person present what he or she has discovered to the group.

CRITICAL*Thinking*

SCANS **ACTIVITY 8-1**

Early in this lesson we discussed the difference between a programming language and a markup language. What are some functions you might want to add to HTML to make it a programming language instead of a markup language? (*Hint:* Repetition and interactivity are the key differences.)

FROM BEGINNING TO END (AND MORE...)

The Importance of Design—A Review

Through the course of this text you've completed the design and production of a Web site. From this work you undoubtedly realize the importance of design. Design allows two things to happen simultaneously that are typically not associated with each other: The quality of the work can be increased while keeping the costs (time and money) relatively under control. Let's take a moment to review what we have learned about Web site design.

Information Design

The first kind of design we discussed was information design. In information design the first three things to consider are the message, the audience, and the purpose of the Web site. These are the foundation of everything you do with the Web site. These three are inexorably tied together; you cannot think about one of them without considering all three. For instance, if you think about WHO the Web site is for (audience), it's hard not to consider WHY you're building the Web site in the first place (purpose) and WHAT it is you'd like to say (message).

Once you've identified message, audience, and purpose, it's time to create the content. This is basically the message in detail. You'll want to decide in advance what you ARE and ARE NOT going to cover—this is called scope. Once you have a rough outline of your content or message, you organize it. You can do this visually with a flowchart like the one shown in Figure 9-1.

FIGURE 9-1
A flowchart

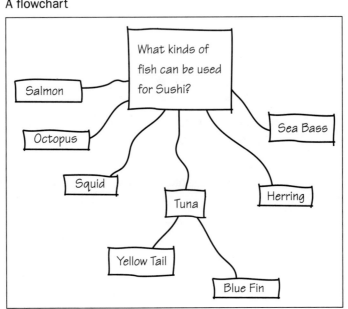

Throughout this book we have consistently recommended testing as you go. This kind of testing is called *formative testing* because you're doing it as you create the site. (The other type, which happens after everything is done, is called *summative testing*.) To test your information design, you want to find out if you've included all the things you should. Content testing involves asking an expert if the information says what it's supposed to say—if you've covered the subject (message) adequately for your audience and purpose.

Interaction Design

When you've finished information design, you pretty much know what your site is going to be about. You then need to think about how the Web site is going to work. We call this interaction design. Looked at another way, interaction design covers two very important things: *functionality* (how the Web site works, such as how you get around in it) and *usability* (whether it is easy to use). You can plan these using a storyboard. A storyboard is very much like an expanded flowchart. Each page is drawn or written on a 3 × 5 card (see Figure 9-2). These cards are then placed on a poster board or on another board, with lines drawn to show the relationships.

FIGURE 9-2
A storyboard card

Just as you tested the information design, you can test the interaction design. Test the functionality with experts by asking if they think it will work. Test the usability with a group by showing them the way the Web site will work, and asking them whether they think it will be easy to use. As with all tests, pay attention to the answers and make adjustments to your design as needed.

Presentation Design

At long last, when you have created a design for all the information and interaction, it is time to decide how the Web site will look. We call this presentation design. Presentation design consists of coming up with visual themes or metaphors to apply to the entire site. A visual theme can be as simple as selecting certain colors, fonts, and graphic elements that will appear on every page to give the site a cohesive look. A metaphor is much more difficult to conjure, but it involves finding an analogy in real life that your audience will understand to make the whole Web site easier to understand and navigate.

What tools can you use to help you construct a good presentation design? Sketches. Specifically thumbnail sketches and rough sketches. Sketches are to an artist what test tubes are to a chemist. They allow you to try things out inexpensively to see which one is going to work. Thumbnail sketches are very small and very inexact, so you can make lots of them in very little time. Rough sketches are developed from a selected thumbnail sketch to refine things a little. A third level not mentioned in the text is a final sketch that more precisely shows the way things are supposed to look.

FIGURE 9-3
A thumbnail sketch and a rough sketch

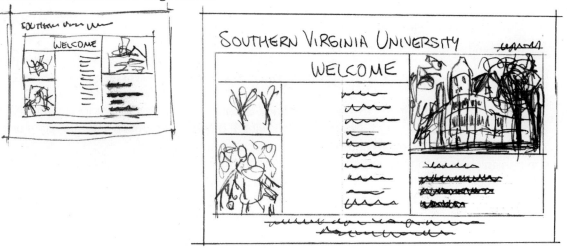

Because the aesthetics of a site are a matter of opinion and style, it is best to put the presentation design in front of several people—preferably members of your audience—to test it. Then, just ask them what they think of it.

STEP-BY-STEP 9.1

1. On a small piece of paper write your name and the following words: **1. Information Design**; **2. Interaction Design**; **3. Presentation Design**; **4. Testing Design**.

2. Partner with a member of your class and explain the meaning of each of the terms. Have your partner check off each term as you explain it, and then initial the paper.

3. Allow yourself to be taught by someone else in your class (not the same person you taught).

4. Compare the explanation you gave to the explanation that was given to you. Did you include everything necessary for a complete explanation? If not, review the appropriate sections of this text and try giving your explanation again.

Programming Skills

DESIGN IN ORDER

Probably the most common error when building a Web site is to start with the presentation design. Because the presentation design has to do with how the final product will look, and because it involves visualizing the final Web site, many designers like to start there; they like the immediate gratification of seeing what the Web site will look like. If you do that, however, you bypass all the information that could make even your graphic theme better. Stick to the order identified in this book: information design first, then interaction design, and then presentation design.

Communication Skills

APPLICATION OF DESIGN TO OTHER THINGS

The process of design described in this book is not limited to Web sites. Nearly any form of communication would benefit from following a process very much like this one. For example, imagine that you've decided to start a school newspaper. How would you adapt the design process to that purpose? Or imagine that your school has decided to start a closed-circuit television station to make announcements. How might you apply this design process to that project? You may even find that the design process will work for very different things too, such as planning a paper, planning a party, or planning a vacation.

Getting It Built—A Review of Production

Unlike design, there is not a specific order for the production of the Web site. Generally, however, the content is contained in the text of the site, so it makes sense to do that first. The pictures usually supplement the text so it makes sense to do them second. And then you can build the entire site when you have all the other elements for the Web site.

Creating Text

The critical thing to remember when creating text for your Web site is the nature of the medium. While the Web is different from paper, television, and many other media, it shares some of the same attributes. Regardless of the medium, people do not usually tolerate long, verbose explanations or descriptions—and this is especially true of Web texts. Like some other media, Web texts usually need to be kept very short and to the point. The word we used in Lesson 6 was *concise*—which is a term you may have heard an English teacher use a time or two.

A second thing to remember is just because you're writing for a new medium does not mean that you can be sloppy or inexact in your writing. Quite the contrary: You should write as well or better than you do for any other medium. Because Web texts are usually short, they have to make their points quickly and get the attention of the reader right off the bat. Not only that, but unlike paper, which may be seen by only a few, the Web can put you in front of the world instantly. Because of that, you'll want to be extra careful about misspellings, grammatical errors, and other sloppy writing. What applies to writing well for paper applies doubly so for the Web.

Producing Graphics

Producing graphics for the Web requires knowledge of a couple of specific limitations that the Web imposes. First, the Web can only handle a couple of specific formats in-line (in the Web browser's window). These are JPEG (sometimes known by the file extension .jpg) and GIF (with the file extension .gif). The JPEG format is particularly good for photographs and other pictures with lots of color detail. The GIF format is good for icons and other graphics without much color information—which you want to load in series, animate, or to have a transparent background. Figure 9-4 shows a Web page that uses a JPEG image.

FIGURE 9-4
A Web page with a graphic

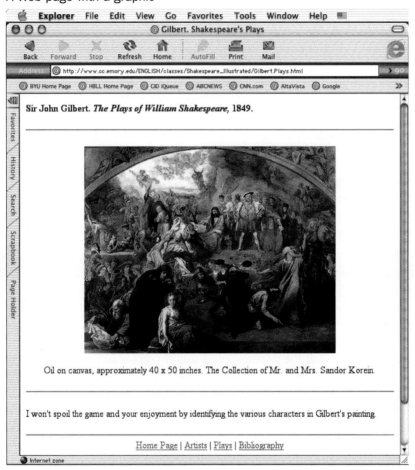

Second, because you want to have your Web page load as quickly as possible, you don't want any wasted bytes. You will want to format your pictures to the exact size needed on the page at 72 *dpi* (dots per inch).

You can use a professional tool like Photoshop to prepare your graphic images, but there are also a number of less expensive tools for doing this work.

Programming

Technically speaking, creating Web pages is a process of markup not programming, but we often hear it referred to as programming anyway. HTML, which, as you may recall, stands for HyperText Markup Language, is the language we use to make Web pages. You do not need a fancy tool to create Web pages—though they certainly make creating HTML a lot easier, especially if you're doing something fancy. You can use any simple text editor (SimpleText, NotePad, or TextEdit) rather than more sophisticated special-purpose programs, or even word processors (Microsoft Word or WordPerfect). Figure 9-5 illustrates the "code" (HTML tags and text) required to create a simple Web page.

FIGURE 9-5
HTML for a simple Web page

```
<HTML>
<HEAD>
<TITLE>Sample HTML</TITLE>
</HEAD>
<BODY bgcolor="gray">
<H1>Just a Little Poem..."</H1>
        <P align="center">Mary had a little lamb<BR>Its fleece was white as
        snow<BR>And everywhere that Mary went<BR>The lamb was sure to
        go</P>
</BODY>
</HTML>
```

Tags are special words that appear in angle brackets (less than and greater than symbols), which are used to tell the browser how to display the text. They can make text bold or italic, place things in paragraphs or tables, insert graphics, or let you link to other Web pages anywhere on the Internet. HTML is a fairly simple language, but its simplicity is what makes it so powerful. Figure 9-6 shows the Web page (as viewed in a browser) that was created with the tags and text shown in Figure 9-5.

FIGURE 9-6
The HTML in Figure 9-5 as displayed in a browser

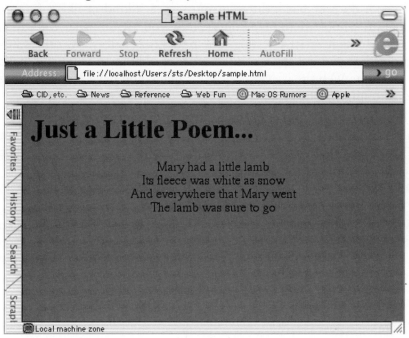

STEP-BY-STEP 9.2

1. On a small piece of paper write your name and the following words: **1. Writing Web Texts**; **2. Preparing Graphics**; **3. HTML Programming**; **4. Testing Production**.

2. Partner with a member of your class and explain the meaning of each of the terms. Have your partner check off each term as you explain it, and then initial the paper.

3. Allow yourself to be taught by someone else in your class (not the same person you taught).

4. Compare the explanation you gave to the explanation that was given to you. Did you include everything necessary for a complete explanation? If not, review the appropriate sections of this text and try giving your explanation again.

Testing Your Web Site—One Last Step

Formative Testing

Now you're done, right? Wrong. Now you have to do what we've been advocating in each of the preceding lessons: Test. You shouldn't be afraid of testing—if you've been following the instructions in this book, you've already done a lot of it. The kind of testing you do at the end is no different from the testing you did during the creation of your Web site, but now it has a different purpose.

The testing you did during the building of your Web site was called formative testing. Its purpose is to help make sure that what you're building is of the highest quality. Hopefully, if you did the testing the way we recommended, it helped you improve your Web site.

Summative Testing

The testing you'll do now has a different purpose. It's kind of like a final grade in a class. Intermittent grades in school are to help you see how you are doing so you can change course if you need to—kind of like formative testing. The final grade is to show others how well you did. It's kind of a proof that you did the work. That's very similar to what summative testing does. Not only that, but if the Web site is ever done over again, you have very good information about what can be done to improve it.

You probably noticed that all the testing we recommended you do involved one of two methods: asking an expert (*expert advice*) and asking a group of people selected from your audience (focus group). The best way to conduct summative testing is to do both again, but for the sake of time, Web designers often limit themselves to just group testing. The thinking is that two heads are better than one—even if one is an expert. So, have a group of people look at your Web site, and then answer questions on a survey.

Basically, you'll take the questions you asked along the way, consolidate them, and make them specific to your Web site. Following is a list of the questions adapted from questions we suggested you ask in formative testing. Use these questions in your summative testing to confirm the quality of your Web site.

- Is this Web site appropriate for its audience?
- Is this Web site's purpose clear?
- Is this Web site's message well organized?

- Can you tell where you are in relation to the whole Web site?

- Is the Web site easy to navigate? Is it easy to find your way around?

- Is this Web site easy to use?

- Is this Web site attractive? Does its look match its message and purpose? Will the audience understand the visual themes and metaphors used?

- Is the text appropriate? Is it clear, correct, and complete?

- Are the pictures appropriate? Do they support the purpose of the Web site adequately? Are they the right size and resolution?

- Does the HTML work? Does it look like it is supposed to and do what it is supposed to?

  Naturally, you'll need to adapt these questions to your own Web site.

One style of survey you can use is called a *Likert scale* (because it was invented by a man named Likert). You've undoubtedly seen these before. To make a Likert questionnaire, convert each question into a statement and then put the numbers 1 through 5 before each statement. The people taking your survey circle a number to indicate how much they agree or disagree with the statement. For example, if you wanted to answer the question "Is the purpose of this Web site clear?" and your Web site was about sushi, you might write the question as shown in Figure 9-7.

FIGURE 9-7
Sample instructions and question for a Web site Likert scale survey

> Instructions: Circle the number that most reflects how you feel.
>   1 = strongly disagree, 5 = strongly agree.
> 1 2 3 4 5   This Web site is obviously about sushi.

S TEP-BY-STEP 9.3

1. Using the summative questions listed in this section, create a Likert scale survey about your Web site that contains at least ten statements. Make the statements apply directly to your Web site.

2. If your Web site has already been produced, have at least five people tour your site and take your survey. Tabulate the results of your survey in a spreadsheet, calculate averages, and draw conclusions from the way these people answered the questions.

Programming Skills

1/3 DESIGN, 1/3 PRODUCTION, 1/3 TESTING

In software engineering, it is common for design and testing (the first part of the process and the very last) to be neglected. A common mistake is to allow for only a little time to design a software product, then to spend lots of time creating it, and then to allocate only a little time to test it. In fact, you should plan on spending one third of your time planning (designing) your Web site, one third of your time building it, and one third of your time testing it. If you do this, your Web site will turn out much better!

SUMMARY

In this lesson you learned:

- How the design process of a Web site is an integration of information design, interaction design, and presentation design.

- That the production of a Web site includes processes such as writing Web texts, manipulating graphics, and programming HTML.

- The differences between formative and summative testing, and how to prepare a survey to conduct summative testing.

VOCABULARY *Review*

Define the following terms:

dpi	Functionality	Summative testing
Expert advice	Likert scale	Usability
Formative testing		

REVIEW *Questions*

TRUE/FALSE

Circle T if the statement is true or F if the statement is false.

T   F   1. A flowchart is part of presentation design.

T   F   2. Graphic elements must be prepared using HTML.

T   F   3. Making rough sketches is a valuable tool for presentation design.

T   F   4. It is vital that Web texts be short and to the point.

T   F   5. Information design uses storyboards to define the information.

FILL IN THE BLANK

Complete the following sentences by writing the correct word or words in the blanks provided.

1. Three pieces of information you should identify in the information design are _____ _____, and _____.

2. Two things to consider when doing interaction design are _____ and _____.

3. Determining the look of your Web site is part of _____ design.

4. Your goal for your Web site's text should be to make it accurate and _____.

5. The two graphics formats (or file types) typically used for Web pictures are _____ and _____.

WRITTEN QUESTIONS

Write a brief answer to each of the following questions.

1. What is a flowchart and how is it used?

2. What is a storyboard. How do you use a storyboard?

3. What is the difference between thumbnail and rough sketches? Explain how you'd use them to help you with your design.

4. What are the two main ways to conduct various tests on a Web site?

5. Create an example of a Likert scale question.

PROJECTS

PROJECT 9-1

You have mentioned to your employer that you have Web design skills. She has decided to give you an opportunity to design her Web site, but she wants some assurance that you really have the skills you say you have. She asks you to write a plan of exactly what you're going to do for her. (If you are not currently employed, you may substitute the president of a club or a coach of a school team.)

PROJECT 9-2

Having built the Web site described in Project 9-1, your employer now would like some assurance that the quality of your work is high. She has given you permission to survey other employees to test the Web site and to ensure its quality. Make up a survey using at least 10 Likert scale statements to give to your test group.

TEAMWORK PROJECT

As a team, select a Web site of local interest, such as a school Web site or that of a local business. Using the questions in the section of this lesson titled Testing Your Web Site—One Last Step discuss among the team the quality of the Web site you have chosen. Using an A-B-C-D-F grade, have the team come to a consensus and give the Web site a grade.

CRITICAL *Thinking*

SCANS ACTIVITY 9-1

Below is a memo from Mr. Traferri, the Special Projects Director, to you, the Creative Director of the Enterprise Web Development team. Write a memo that responds to Mr. Traferri's concerns.

MEMO

From: Marco Traferri, Special Projects Director

To: Creative Director, Enterprise Web Development team

We appreciate your taking charge of developing our company's Web site. As you are aware, we are profitable this quarter but not as much as we have been in previous quarters. Because of this we are looking for things we can cut. In looking over your Web site plans, I noticed that you planned and budgeted for summative testing. I am uncertain of the need for this. Please explain how summative testing will benefit either the Web site or the company as a whole. We need this information before we can approve your plan and budget.

PRODUCING YOUR WEB SITE

REVIEW *Questions*

TRUE/FALSE

Circle T if the statement is true or F if the statement is false.

T F   1. HTML stands for HyperText Markup Language.

T F   2. Aliasing is a process of placing different colored pixels next to each other to represent a third color.

T F   3. Summative testing is used to determine the quality of a finished Web site.

T F   4. To help move things in the right direction as you build a Web site, use formative testing.

T F   5. Dithering is used to make jagged computer font characters look smooth.

T F   6. Pixels are the smallest units of computer graphics representing each "dot" on the screen.

T F   7. RGB stands for Red-Green-Blue.

T F   8. Use the <HR> tag to put a separating line between parts of your Web page.

T F   9. Use nesting to connect one Web document with another.

T F 10. A focus group is a bunch of experts whom you gather to give you advice.

MATCHING

Match the correct term in Column 1 to its description in Column 2.

Column 1	Column 2

—— 1. GIF

A. Cards representing each Web page in a site

—— 2. JPEG

B. The first test software (such as HTML) is put through

—— 3. dpi

C. A measure of graphic resolution

—— 4. functionality

D. A particular "look" applied to a Web site

—— 5. usability

E. A graphic format for photographs

—— 6. visual themes

F. A drawing with boxes showing structure of a Web site

—— 7. metaphors

G. Testing software for final release

—— 8. flowchart

H. When the image on the screen is like something else

—— 9. storyboard

I. A graphics format best used for icons

—— 10. beta testing

J. How a Web site works

K. How easy a Web site is to navigate

WRITTEN QUESTIONS

Write a brief answer to each of the following questions.

1. What tag would you use to link one Web page to another? Explain the tag and give an example.

2. What are a few of the roles that graphics can play on a Web page?

3. What are the three parts of design? List them in order, and briefly describe them.

4. How are HTML tags used to create a Web page?

5. What is the difference between additive and subtractive color? Give an example of each.

6. How are flowcharts and storyboards similar and how are they different?

7. What is the difference between alpha testing and beta testing?

8. What is the difference between formative testing and summative testing?

PROJECTS

In this book we have proposed a process for design in which the Web developer starts with information design (audience, purpose, message, structure); then conducts interaction design (functionality, usability, navigation); and then conducts presentation design (visual themes and metaphors). We also recommend conducting the actual work of the Web site in the order given in these lessons: Web text (the text in all pages), graphics, and encoding into HTML (programming). The following projects have to do with the order in which these are done.

SCANS **PROJECT 1**

Think about doing the design in a different order (such as doing interaction design first). What would be the ramifications of changing the order? (Given the changed order, explain what would happen if you tried to do things in that order.) Summarize by explaining the outcome of inverting the order.

SCANS **PROJECT 2**

Think about doing the production work in a different order (for example, doing HTML programming first). What would be the ramifications of changing the order? (Given the changed order, explain what would happen if you tried to do things in that order.) Summarize by explaining the outcome of inverting the order.

CRITICAL *Thinking*

In this book we have used two methods to test Web pages, content, interaction, and so forth. The two methods are expert advice and a focus group made up of members of your audience.

SCANS **ACTIVITY 1**

Identify the strengths and weaknesses of each method of testing Web pages.

SCANS **ACTIVITY 2**

Go back through the book and identify all the different kinds of tests (evaluations) that we suggested (these are usually the last sections in each lesson). Analyze these and explain why an expert is more valuable in some instances and a focus group in others. What general principles determine whether to use one or the other?

UNDERSTANDING RGB AND HEXADECIMAL FOR WEB-SAFE COLORS

What Is Hexadecimal?

Computers are binary devices. That means that they deal most easily with numbers that are powers of two. For example, at a fundamental level, 2, 4, 8, 16, 32, and so on are handled much more easily than the decimal numbers we are used to: 1, 10, 100, 1,000, and so on, which are powers of ten.

In order to accommodate this preference for powers of two, computers sometimes use a different numbering scheme from base 10. One common scheme is base 16. The technical term for base 16 is *hexadecimal.*

To write hexadecimal numbers, we use the digits 0 through 9 for the numbers zero through nine, just as in regular form. After that, we need some kind of single-digit characters to represent numbers 10 through 15. Computer scientists have substituted the letters A through F for those numbers. Therefore, counting to 15 in hexadecimal is 1, 2, 3, 4, 5, 6, 7, 8, 9, A, B, C, D, E, and F.

In a normal decimal system, the first column of numbers is the "ones" column, and the second is the "tens" column. In a hexadecimal system, the first column is the "ones" column, and the second is the "sixteens" column. When you count in hexadecimal, you count up to 15 (using letters from A thru F for the extra digits). When you reach sixteen, you place a 1 in the "sixteens" column and start the "ones" column over. So counting to 27 in hexadecimal would look like this: 1, 2, 3, 4, 5, 6, 7, 8, 9, A, B, C, D, E, F, 10, 11, 12, 13, 14, 15, 16, 17, 18, 19, 1A, 1B. The hexadecimal "number" 1B equals the decimal number 27.

In Table A-1, the numbers counting from 0 to 255 (in decimal) are shown in both decimal and hexadecimal form, with decimal on the left and hexadecimal on the right.

TABLE A-1
0 to 255 in decimal and hexadecimal form

0 = 00	32 = 20	64 = 40	96 = 60	128 = 80	160 = A0	192 = C0	224 = E0
1 = 01	33 = 21	65 = 41	97 = 61	129 = 81	161 = A1	193 = C1	225 = E1
2 = 02	34 = 22	66 = 42	98 = 62	130 = 82	162 = A2	194 = C2	226 = E2
3 = 03	35 = 23	67 = 43	99 = 63	131 = 83	163 = A3	195 = C3	227 = E3
4 = 04	36 = 24	68 = 44	100 = 64	132 = 84	164 = A4	196 = C4	228 = E4
5 = 05	37 = 25	69 = 45	101 = 65	133 = 85	165 = A5	197 = C5	229 = E5
6 = 06	38 = 26	70 = 46	102 = 66	134 = 86	166 = A6	198 = C6	230 = E6
7 = 07	39 = 27	71 = 47	103 = 67	135 = 87	167 = A7	199 = C7	231 = E7
8 = 08	40 = 28	72 = 48	104 = 68	136 = 88	168 = A8	200 = C8	232 = E8
9 = 09	41 = 29	73 = 49	105 = 69	137 = 89	169 = A9	201 = C9	233 = E9
10 = 0A	42 = 2A	74 = 4A	106 = 6A	138 = 8A	170 = AA	202 = CA	234 = EA
11 = 0B	43 = 2B	75 = 4B	107 = 6B	139 = 8B	171 = AB	203 = CB	235 = EB
12 = 0C	44 = 2C	76 = 4C	108 = 6C	140 = 8C	172 = AC	204 = CC	236 = EC
13 = 0D	45 = 2D	77 = 4D	109 = 6D	141 = 8D	173 = AD	205 = CD	237 = ED
14 = 0E	46 = 2E	78 = 4E	110 = 6E	142 = 8E	174 = AE	206 = CE	238 = EE
15 = 0F	47 = 2F	79 = 4F	111 = 6F	143 = 8F	175 = AF	207 = CF	239 = EF
16 = 10	48 = 30	80 = 50	112 = 70	144 = 90	176 = B0	208 = D0	240 = F0
17 = 11	49 = 31	81 = 51	113 = 71	145 = 91	177 = B1	209 = D1	241 = F1
18 = 12	50 = 32	82 = 52	114 = 72	146 = 92	178 = B2	210 = D2	242 = F2
19 = 13	51 = 33	83 = 53	115 = 73	147 = 93	179 = B3	211 = D3	243 = F3
20 = 14	52 = 34	84 = 54	116 = 74	148 = 94	180 = B4	212 = D4	244 = F4
21 = 15	53 = 35	85 = 55	117 = 75	149 = 95	181 = B5	213 = D5	245 = F5
22 = 16	54 = 36	86 = 56	118 = 76	150 = 96	182 = B6	214 = D6	246 = F6
23 = 17	55 = 37	87 = 57	119 = 77	151 = 97	183 = B7	215 = D7	247 = F7
24 = 18	56 = 38	88 = 58	120 = 78	152 = 98	184 = B8	216 = D8	248 = F8
25 = 19	57 = 39	89 = 59	121 = 79	153 = 99	185 = B9	217 = D9	249 = F9
26 = 1A	58 = 3A	90 = 5A	122 = 7A	154 = 9A	186 = BA	218 = DA	250 = FA
27 = 1B	59 = 3B	91 = 5B	123 = 7B	155 = 9B	187 = BB	219 = DB	251 = FB
28 = 1C	60 = 3C	92 = 5C	124 = 7C	156 = 9C	188 = BC	220 = DC	252 = FC
29 = 1D	61 = 3D	93 = 5D	125 = 7D	157 = 9D	189 = BD	221 = DD	253 = FD
30 = 1E	62 = 3E	94 = 5E	126 = 7E	158 = 9E	190 = BE	222 = DE	254 = FE
31 = 1F	63 = 3F	95 = 5F	127 = 7F	159 = 9F	191 = BF	223 = DF	255 = FF

What Does Hexadecimal Numbering Have to Do with Color?

As stated, computers deal in binary numbers. So, representation of color on a computer is also in binary numbers.

To represent the 16-million-plus colors that the human eye can distinguish, computer scientists have come up with a clever scheme that connects the hexadecimal numbers above to each of the three primary additive colors (see Lesson 8), red, green, and blue (RGB for short).

Imagine three dials or knobs, one for each color (see Figure A-1). As you turn the dial to the right, it represents a higher number; as you turn it to the left, it represents a lower number. The numbers are between 0 and 255 (or, in hexadecimal, between 0 and FF).

FIGURE A-1
Color dials

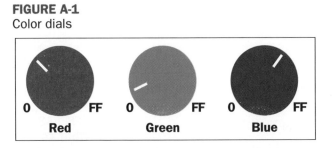

With these three imaginary knobs, you can create any color. For example, to create a pure red, you simply turn the Red knob all the way to the right (to FF) and the other two all the way to the left (to 00). To create a pure blue, turn the Blue knob all the way to the right (FF) and the other two knobs all the way to the left (00).

What if you want a darker blue? Just turn the Blue knob down a little, and you have a darker color.

What about white? Turn all three knobs all the way to "FF."

What if you want yellow? As mentioned in Lesson 7, with additive colors, yellow is a product of adding red and green. Therefore, turn the Red and Green knobs all the way to the right and the Blue knob all the way to the left.

Using RGB with hexadecimal numbers is exactly how the Web designates colors. Instead of turning knobs, however, you put six hexadecimal digits all in a row preceded by a pound sign (#) to show that it's a number. The first two digits represent red, the second two indicate green, and the third two represent blue. So for pure red, you would key #FF0000. For pure blue, you would key #0000FF, and for pure green you would key #00FF00. In this system, #FFFF00 would give you pure yellow.

What Are "Web-Safe" Colors?

If all the computers in the world could handle millions of colors, this would work perfectly. Unfortunately, there are some that can only display 256 colors. So, just to be safe, we select only 256 of the millions of possible colors for use on the Web. (Actually, we select 216—the other 32 "color slots" are saved for the operating systems to add their own colors.)

How do we choose the 216 colors? Netscape devised a simple trick (which the industry has accepted as the standard) to decide which colors to choose. They use *only* doubled numbers that are divisible by three in each of the positions (R, G, and B).

These numbers are: 00   33   66   99   CC   FF

In decimal numbers, these values would be 0, 51, 102, 153, 204, and 255 (see Table A-1). This gives you six choices for each primary color: red, green, and blue. That means that, instead of having $256 \times 256 \times 256$ (= 16,777,216) different colors, you only have $6 \times 6 \times 6$ (= 216) different colors. These 216 possible colors are the "safe" colors.

The best way to see these colors is to try them out in your HTML code. Use the rule above to change the background color of a Web page and view it in your browser to see the colors. The background color is modified by adding the BGCOLOR= argument to your body tag, like this:

<BODY BGCOLOR="FFFF00">

The above tag would make the background bright yellow.

<BODY BGCOLOR="99FF99">

The tag above would make a light, pastel green (the addition of the other two colors, red and blue, in equal amounts adds "white" to the color, making it lighter).

Try your own combinations.

Extra Challenge

Can you tell which of the following numbers are "Web-safe" colors and which are not?
#3366CC   #000077
#FFFF33   #DDCC33
What colors do you think these represent?

Extra for Experts

There are a variety of Web sites that show the color palette of Web-safe colors and their hexadecimal equivalent. You can use the Internet and the search tool of your browser to find these sites by searching for keywords such as "hexadecimal," "Web-safe colors," or "color palette."

APPENDIX B

GLOSSARY OF HTML

The following glossary is not a complete set for HTML. It is provided here as a convenience for identifying some of the most common HTML terms.

HTML is the set of tags and other entities used to "mark up" a document for display on a Web browser.

In the glossary, tags are listed with their purpose or meaning. Some common attributes may also be listed. The tags are organized into types of tags (not alphabetically), which assumes that you know something about tags and the structure of an HTML document.

The words to the right of each tag refer to whether the tag requires a closing tag and whether the tag has attributes.

Document Tags

A standard HTML document contains tags that identify parts of the document itself. These are <HEAD> and <BODY>. Those items between the opening and closing <HEAD> tag are not displayed in the user's browser, but are read by it and used in other ways. The content between the <BODY> tags is displayed in the browser window, if possible.

One of the most common elements of the <HEAD> is the <TITLE> tag, which appears in the browser window's title (above the window—not in the window itself).

Surrounding both of these are the <HTML> tags that identify the entire document as being HTML. The typical arrangement for an HTML document is as follows (some items have been indented to make them easier to follow):

```
<HTML>
    <HEAD>
        <TITLE>The Window Title</TITLE>
    </HEAD>
    <BODY>
        [The page's content goes here...]
    </BODY>
</HTML>
```

Text Breaks, Lines, and Layout

| <P> | Paragraph | Closing Tag: Optional | Attributes: Optional |

The equivalent of putting two returns after a paragraph, the paragraph tag leaves a blank line. The <P> tag has an optional closing tag (</P>). We recommend using the closing tag so that formatting attributes can be added to the opening tag. For example: <P ALIGN="RIGHT">*Text*</P> will right-align the text between the tags.

|
 | Break | Closing Tag: None | Attributes: None |

The line break tag is the equivalent of putting one return after a paragraph: there is no blank line between paragraphs. The <BR> tag does not require a closing tag. Also, <BR> tags can be "stacked" or multiplied to cause multiple spaces between paragraphs.

| <HR> | Horizontal Rule | Closing Tag: None | Attributes: Some |

The terminology for this tag comes from the print industry where a line drawn in the text is called a rule. The <HR> tag does not require a closing tag. The tag can contain attributes that vary the width of the line drawn and whether the line has a drop shadow or not (WIDTH="4" and NOSHADE, respectively).

Text Style Tags

Text styles fall into two categories: logical and physical. When the Web was first conceived, its purpose was to share scientific papers. Consequently, many tags were created that were based on the logical structure of text, not the physical look. These logical tags allow the browser to determine how to display tagged text.

Physical tags, on the other hand, are more like the physical display characteristics of a typical word processor and are based on how the text looks. All of the tags below fall into one of these two categories.

| <ADDRESS> | Address | Closing Tag: Required | Attributes: None |

The address tag is a logical text style (one the browser can choose how to display) for writing addresses. This usually indents the text.

| <B> | Boldface | Closing Tag: Required | Attributes: None |

This is a physical style for displaying the surrounded text in boldface.

| <BLOCKQUOTE> | Block Quote | Closing Tag: Required | Attributes: None |

A logical text style for large blocks of quoted material in a text, the block quote tag usually indents the long quotation about one-half inch from both the right and left margins.

| <CITE> | Citation | Closing Tag: Required | Attributes: None |

A logical text style for citations, this tag usually puts the citation in italics.

<CODE>   Computer Code   Closing Tag: Required   Attributes: None

This tag creates a logical text style intended to surround computer code. This usually puts the text in a monospaced font, such as Courier.

<EM>   Emphasis   Closing Tag: Required   Attributes: None

The emphasis tag is a logical text style for giving emphasis to the surrounded text. This usually puts the text into italics.

<FONT>   Font   Closing Tag: Required   Attributes: **Several**

A physical style for changing the font of the surrounded text, the font tag's attributes can include instructions such as SIZE="+2" (make the surrounded text two sizes larger than default) and FACE="HELVETICA,GENEVA,SANSERIF" (use one of the identified font faces). This tag is generally not compatible with older browsers.

<I>   Italics   Closing Tag: Required   Attributes: None

The italics tag is a physical style for displaying the surrounded text in italics.

<PRE>   Preformatted   Closing Tag: Required   Attributes: None

This is a physical style for displaying the surrounded text without any formatting changes. For example, all space characters and the return character are left intact. This usually displays as a monospaced font, such as Courier.

<STRONG>   Strong Emphasis   Closing Tag: Required   Attributes: None

A logical text style for giving strong emphasis to the surrounded text, this tag usually puts the text into boldface.

<TT>   Teletype   Closing Tag: Required   Attributes: None

This is a physical style for displaying the surrounded text in a monospaced font, such as a Teletype or typewriter.

<XMP>   Example   Closing Tag: Required   Attributes: None

A logical text style for displaying HTML code in the browser window, this unique tag usually sets the text in a monospaced font, such as Courier, but also allows all characters that would normally be interpreted to be displayed, such as less than (<), greater than (>), ampersand (&), and so on.

Page Layout Tags

<CENTER>   Center   Closing Tag: Required   Attributes: None

Although not strictly a text style tag, <CENTER> affects all the text between it and its closing tag (</CENTER>) by centering the text on the page. It has no attributes.

<H1>   Level 1 Heading   Closing Tag: Required   Attributes: None

A top-level heading, this is usually displayed at a large point size and in boldface.

<H2>   Level 2 Heading   Closing Tag: Required   Attributes: None

A second-level heading, this is usually displayed at a large point size and in boldface (but smaller than <H1>).

<H3> through <H6> Other Headings   Closing Tags: Required   Attributes: None

These tags create third- through sixth-level headings, each smaller than the previous heading.

<TABLE>   Table   Closing Tag: Required   Attributes: None

The <TABLE> tag is used to surround text that is to be formatted as a table. The following two additional tags should be included within the opening and closing table tags.

<TR>   Table Row   Closing Tag: Required   Attributes: Some

Use the <TR> tag to surround things to be in the same row in a table. These should be inside a set of <TABLE> tags.

<TD>   Table Cell   Closing Tag: Required   Attributes: Several

Use the <TD> tag to surround each cell (or column) in a table. These should be inside a set of <TR> tags, which should be inside a set of <TABLE> tags.

Tables are powerful ways to lay out your Web pages attractively. For more information on using tables in HTML, use your favorite search engine to find sites related to HTML tables, or check the Web page for this book, which can be found at the Course Web site (*http://www.course.com*) by searching for this book by its title or ISBN number.

Lists

Some of the most flexible and useful tags are those that allow you to create lists. Lists usually take two sets of tags, one to surround the entire list and another to surround each of the items in the list. Unless otherwise stated, the list item tag is <LI>, which has an optional closing tag and can take attributes (depending on the list type).

<OL>   Ordered List   Closing Tag: Required   Attributes: Some

The ordered list uses the <OL> tag on each item in the list. When displayed in the browser, a number is displayed at the beginning of each line referenced to the order in which that line appears.

<UL>   Unordered List   Closing Tag: Required   Attributes: Some

An unordered list uses the <UL> tag on each item in the list. When displayed in the browser, a bullet (•) is displayed at the beginning of each line.

<DL> Definition List Closing Tag: Required Attributes: None

The definition list is a unique way to have the contents in the list vary between two different list item types. Use the tag <DT> for the "definition title" and <DD> for the "definition." This tag is particularly useful for glossaries, dictionaries, or other types of entries where you want indentation to show the relationship between items in the list.

Inline Graphics

<IMG> Image Closing Tag: Required Attributes: Required

The <IMG> tag must have an attribute to identify the filename and location of the image to be displayed. This is done using the attribute SRC="*url*". In addition, other attributes (such as HEIGHT="24" or WIDTH="322") are also possible. See the following section on anchors for more detail on how to use the URL in the quotation marks.

Anchors (Hyperlinks)

<A> Anchor (hyperlink) Closing Tag: Required Attributes: Required

This is the tag that creates the most excitement. The text or graphic surrounded by <A> tags is "hot" and can be clicked to take the user to a new location on the Web. The location is determined by the contents of the attribute HREF="*url*".

<A> Anchor (target) Closing Tag: Required Attributes: Required

There is a second use of the <A> tag that makes it the recipient (not the sender) of a link. Using the <A NAME="#*anyname*"> tag, you can get to a specific place *within* an HTML document, not just to its top. When a URL contains a pound sign ("#"), the words after the pound sign are treated as the target of a link within an HTML document.

GLOSSARY

A

Additive color The method of creating images on a computer screen by combining different colors of light.

Aliasing The stair-step effect caused by square pixels on a computer screen.

Alpha testing The first testing that software is put through, usually by the programmer.

Anchor tag In HTML, a link to another Web page.

Angle brackets A less-than sign ("<") and greater-than sign (">") used as brackets for HTML tags.

Anti-aliasing Shading pixels on the border of an aliased image to give the appearance of smoothness.

Attributes An addition to an HTML tag that modifies how the tag will work. Attributes are placed inside the beginning tag.

Audience The group of people for whom a Web site is designed.

B

Background Colors or images that appear behind the main elements of a Web page.

Balance Arranging objects on the page so that they look to be of equal "weight" around an imaginary center line.

Banner A headline or text-art logo that appears across the top or along the side of a Web page. This is usually the name of the Web site.

Beta testing A more thorough testing done by someone other than the programmer.

Body text The part of the text that contains the main information. Body text is usually the text found in the middle of the paragraph.

Breakdown Subdividing a large job (such as building a Web site) into smaller tasks.

Bullet In typography, a round dot used to make a line stand out.

C

Chunks Divisions or pieces of information. These are often built out of existing content that is "broken up" into chunks.

Color depth The number of bits used to represent a color; 8-bit color has a palette of 256 colors.

Concise Clear and brief writing that gets right to the point.

Conclusion That part of the text that finishes the thoughts that the text is addressing and ties everything together; usually the last sentence.

Consistency errors Errors caused by switching from one tense to another or from one set of pronouns to another. Using contractions in one part of the text and not in another is a common consistency error.

Content testing Testing to see if the content is there and correct.

Context device Any graphic element used to help the user recognize what "context" they are in; for example, a distinctive logo that appears on every page.

D

Design document A document whose purpose is to guide the production of a Web site.

Dithering Making a limited number of colors look like more by placing related colors next to each other in a pattern.

Document tag HTML tags that surround an entire document.

Downloading Moving files from a server to a client computer; also, moving a file to a browser from a Web server.

dpi (dots per inch) A measurement of graphic resolution. 72 dpi is a common synonym for screen resolution.

E

Educated guess A process of breaking down the task (building a Web site) into smaller tasks, estimating their cost and time, and then adding them all together.

Ending tag Many HTML tags come in pairs. The ending tag usually has a slash ("/") inside the angle brackets.

Expert advice A form of testing or evaluation that involves seeking input from a knowledgeable person.

F

Flowchart A visual aid in understanding the organization of information's "flow." It is usually made up of boxes connected by lines, where each box represents a Web page or "chunk" of information.

Focus group A form of testing or evaluation where you seek input from a group of people, preferably from your intended audience. In this method, you have a group discuss their likes and dislikes (or some other research question) and make note of their answers.

Formative testing Testing or evaluation conducted during production that is intended to improve output of the final product.

Functional testing Testing to see if the programming works.

Functionality How well a Web site works.

G

GIF CompuServe's "Graphic Interchange Format," a graphics format best for small 8-bit graphics.

Greeking Substitution of a straight or squiggly line for text in a sketch.

GUI (Graphical User Interface) A way of interacting with a computer using icons, windows, and a mouse.

H

Heading An element of a page indicating the beginning of unique content, usually text.

Hierarchical structure A structure, like a pedigree chart, where a single entity has several children, each of which can also have children.

Horizontal rule In typography, a horizontal line between paragraphs.

HTML (HyperText Markup Language) The set of tags in which Web pages are programmed.

HTML tags The principle component of HTML, used to mark up a document.

HTTP (HyperText Transfer Protocol) The way HTML (Web) pages are transmitted to the browser.

Hyperlink A connection between one Web document and another that, when clicked, takes the browser to the second document.

I

Icon Small symbolic graphics, often used as part of the user interface.

Information design The method of determining the information to be included on a Web site, including who it's for (audience), what to say (message), and why to say it (purpose).

Inline graphic Any graphic or media that can appear inside the browser window.

Interaction design That aspect of design where the functionality (how it works) and usability (ease of use) are considered.

Interactivity The actions taken by a user of a Web site or other software as he or she manipulates the content.

Internet The international interconnections between networks on which the World Wide Web's pages are transported.

J

JPEG The graphic format invented by the Joint Photographers Exchange Group, best for high-resolution, high-color graphics such as photographs.

L

Likert scale A survey question in the form of a statement with some numbers before it (most often 1 through 5) that the person taking the survey is to circle to express the degree of agreement (such as "Circle 1 if you completely disagree." or "Circle 5 if you completely agree.").

Linear structure A structure where each step or entity is followed by a single entity in a line.

Link   A connection between one Web document and another that, when clicked, takes the browser to the second document.

Look (noun)   How a Web site looks; the style and appearance of the Web site.

M

Markup language   A kind of computer language that is used to modify the way text looks rather than make the computer perform some other function.

Message   A part of information design that identifies the exact content to be placed on the Web page; what the Web site is about.

Metadata   Data about data, such as the information about a Web page found in its header.

Metaphor   When something stands for something else, such as the trash representing the delete function; an analogy that helps users navigate or manipulate the content of a Web site.

Mixed structure   A mixture of structures; a structure made up of attributes of linear, hierarchical, and random access structures combined.

Modem   A device for translating digital data into tones so they can be transmitted over plain old telephone lines.

N

Navigation   How users of the Web site move among the pages.

Navigation bar   A design element where all the navigation buttons (such as "Previous" and "Next") are grouped together in a "bar."

Nesting   Use of multiple tags on a piece of text in the proper order. The proper order is first-in, last-out.

O

Opening   That part of the text that introduces the subject; usually the first sentence.

Ordered list   A set of HTML tags that places text in a list with numbers at the beginning of each item.

Organization   How the content of a Web site is structured or put together; its structure.

P

Packet   What Internet messages are broken into and then reassembled to transmit.

Palette   A limited number of colors assigned to numbers to allow for color in a Web page picture.

Path   A way of indicating the categories and sub-categories navigated to reach a certain point.

Persona   An imaginary person representative of the audience.

Pixel   (PICture ELements) The smallest "dot" on a computer screen.

Proofread   Reading the text to look for grammatical errors, spelling errors, punctuation errors, etc. This is often performed on the final draft to catch errors that were missed in earlier edits.

Proportion   Sizing objects so that they look like they belong together.

Purpose   A part of information design that identifies the goal or aim of a Web site; the reason the Web site is being created.

R

Random access structure   A structure where every element or entity is accessible from every other element.

Representation   The ability of pictures to represent a real object.

Resolution   How many dots or pixels in an inch. Computer screens have approximately between 72 and 96.

RGB   (Red-Green-Blue) The primary additive colors; also a format of color for computers.

Rough draft   A first attempt to write a text. The rough draft is usually polished, edited, and refined before it becomes a final draft.

Rough sketch   A simple drawing used to make preliminary judgments about the "look" of a Web site. Usually slightly more developed than a thumbnail sketch.

S

Sans serif   Any font lacking in "serifs," which are small cross-lines to major lines in the letters.

Scope statement A statement of how much content the Web site will cover.

Search engine A Web service that indiscriminately searches through Web sites to create a searchable index of Web sites. This differs from a Web index in that it is automated.

Self-contained text When something does not rely on anything else to be understood, it is "self-contained." In text found on Web pages, self-contained means that the text does not rely on information that appears on any other page.

Spell check A function of most word processors that compares each word to a dictionary to see if the word is spelled correctly. Spell checking does not catch correctly spelled words when they are used incorrectly.

Storyboard A visual aid that can be used to organize a Web site for the purpose of clarifying navigation and other interaction issues. It usually takes the form of a collection of 3" × 5" (or other sized) cards placed on a board.

Subtractive color Color acquired by mixing different colors of pigment, as in paint.

Summative testing Testing or evaluation to pass final judgment on a Web site.

Symbols Graphic images that sometimes have abstract meanings; for example, a stop sign.

T

Thumbnail sketch A small, very loosely drawn sketch used to make preliminary judgments about the "look" of a Web site. Their advantage is that several can be made very quickly for comparison.

Tiled When images in a background repeat themselves like floor tile, often forming a pattern.

U

Unity When all the objects on a page look like they belong together.

Unordered list A set of HTML tags that place text in a list with a bullet at the beginning of each item.

URL (Uniform or Universal Resource Locator) A Web address.

Usability How easy a Web site is to use.

Usability testing Testing to see how easy a Web page or site is to use.

V

Visual theme A selection of colors, fonts, graphics, etc. to help create a consistent "look" and "feel" to a Web site.

W

Wayfinding The art of making it easy for users to find their way around something, such as a library or Web site.

Web browser The computer software used to look at Web pages and "browse" from one to another.

Web index A hand-built index of Web pages that is generally categorized for easy access to Web pages. This differs from a search engine in that its principal index has not been built with automation.

Web page The basic part of a Web site; the material viewed in a single Web browser window at one time.

Web server A computer whose job it is to distribute Web pages.

Web site A collection of Web pages, typically from the same server or domain; usually with a common purpose, audience, or message.

Welcome page An opening page intended to welcome visitors to a Web site.

World Wide Web One of several uses of the Internet, made up of World Wide Web pages; often abbreviated WWW.

INDEX